CALLED TO TEACH

CALLED TO TEACH

Ideas and Encouragement for Teachers in the Church

Kent L. Johnson

AUGSBURG Publishing House • Minneapolis

CALLED TO TEACH
Ideas and Encouragement for Teachers in the Church

Copyright © 1984 Augsburg Publishing House

Scripture quotations unless otherwise noted are from the Revised Standard Version of the Bible, copyright 1946, 1952, and 1971 by the Division of Christian Education of the National Council of Churches.

Library of Congress Cataloging in Publication Data

Johnson, Kent L., 1934-
    CALLED TO TEACH.

    Bibliography: p 127
    1. Sunday-school teachers.   I. Title.
BV1534.J64 1984   268   83-72127
ISBN 0-8066-2071-4

Manufactured in the U.S.A.   APH 10-0964

4   5   6   7   8   9   0   1   2   3   4   5   6   7   8   9

To all those in the church
who have been my teachers

Contents

Introduction

"Let not many of you become teachers."　　　*James 3:1*

As far as I know, no one has ever appealed to the epistle of James as a resource for selecting and training teachers for a congregation's educational program. The reason might be that in his clearest words of advice on the subject James wrote: "Let not many of you become teachers, my brethren, for you know that we who teach shall be judged with greater strictness" (James 3:1). That doesn't seem to be a very positive approach for those desperately looking for someone to teach a seventh-grade Sunday school class. In fact, what could be better for those wanting to excuse themselves from the demanding work of teaching than to have a biblical basis for that decision?

On the other hand, for those who want an opportunity to serve and who recognize the challenges that face the church today, these words of James are a call to ministry. Rather than pointing a way out of responsibility, James illustrates the tremendous importance of teachers for the life of the church and the need for those teachers to be faithful to their calling.

9

Anyone who has taken the time to observe a baby is conscious of the importance of teachers. Babies come into the world with few instincts about how to survive. In the first few hours, days, and even years, they are dependent on others for their well-being. In a way, that's the price humans pay for the privilege of being able to learn. Almost from the moment we are born the learning process begins. What and how we learn depends on those who teach us. From our earliest years we have been influenced by others: our parents, our brothers and sisters, friends, and those we call our teachers.

It's awesome to think that one can be involved in the shaping of another's life. Some, such as parents and family members, usually can't avoid it. Teachers, however, are those who have chosen to assume that role in the lives of others. Making that decision implies that teachers have thought about the influence they have on others and are willing to be responsible in exercising it.

Those who teach in the church find that responsibility rooted in the gospel of Jesus Christ. Being in Christ was no small matter for James. It made all the difference. Unless teachers were willing to locate their calling and responsibility there, it was far better that they not teach. James also recognized the tremendous potential of teachers to affect the lives of others. Only in faithfulness to the gospel would their influence contribute to the life of the church and the well-being of those who learn.

James was not alone among the New Testament writers in his concern for teachers and what they taught. The struggle to clarify the faith of the church is evident in the New Testament from Matthew to Revelation. Whether they be true or false, teachers were always a part of that struggle. One of the books that brings this out clearly is the second epistle of Peter. It was written for the purpose of countering the effects of false teachers, and encouraging the efforts of those who confessed faith in Jesus Christ.

Until a year or so ago I had not studied 2 Peter in any great detail. However, after we had completed a study of 1 Peter, the adult class I teach suggested that we go on to study 2 Peter. As we got into it, I discovered that 2 Peter expresses one person's understanding of a Christian teacher. While he wrestled with the effects of false teachers on his readers, the author also described a purpose for Christian education, some ways in which people learn, and the qualities that characterize a true teacher.

The context in which, and to which, 2 Peter was written was not unlike our own. It was written at a time when the phrase "it all depends on where you're coming from" could have been as common as it is today. The church of the first century existed in a pluralistic and diverse society which had the capacity to bring intense pressure on anyone who attempted to hold to convictions about truth—both with respect to doctrine and behavior. The most honored truth of the times could have been that there was no truth. False teachers within the church had difficulty believing that life had much meaning beyond what persons could make for themselves in the present. Claiming to have been set free by Christ to live as they pleased, some of these teachers recognized no constraints on their behavior. Against those claims the writer of 2 Peter affirmed the purposes of God and maintained that God's purposes were being achieved in the hearts and lives of people. The author argued that our lives are an integrated whole—that faith and life are a part of the same fabric. And, like James, he acknowledged the tremendous potential of teachers to influence others. He was concerned that teachers exercise that potential in faithful service to Christ.

A second characteristic we seem to share with the first century is a disinterest in "the last things." These last things include the belief in the return of Christ in glory, salvation, and judgment. There are several things that may contribute to this neglect in our day. Wealth and the good life it can buy has a way of focusing one's attention on the present. "This is the day that counts" is the message to which one is conditioned today—and it was a common message of the first century. The author of 2 Peter addresses this issue by calling people to faith—and particularly to trust in the second coming of the Lord Jesus.

Now, as then, the competitors for the allegiance of people are numerous and strong. The diversity of opinions about truth, with a consequent demand of equality for all views, seems to be characteristic of our time. In these times, how is the church to understand its calling? And in which direction will the church move in the ministry of the gospel? The answers to these questions may well depend on who the teachers of the church are and on what and how they teach. The church today needs able and faithful teachers as much as it did 1900 years ago. The people for this ministry are present in the church. The resources for equipping them are also available. Perhaps the most pressing issue is whether or not these people and resources will come together in educational ministry.

The letter of 2 Peter can help us in finding, equipping, and supporting the teachers our congregations need. Peter's statement of purpose can serve as a point of departure for discussing what each teacher and congregation is about in Christian education. The knowledge that he saw as basic to Christian faith raises for us the question of what knowledge we think has the greatest value for Christians today. The qualities he commends for the Christian teacher can stimulate us to look for people we think can serve the church well as teachers. Peter's concern for fidelity to the truth forces us to examine our understanding of the gospel and how we communicate it to others. The seriousness with which he views the ministry of teaching can stimulate us to evaluate our own enthusiasm and commitment to the gospel, to the office of teacher, and to those we teach. All of this can't but help the educational ministry of a congregation —and the life and mission of the church as well.

For those readers who are presently teachers, I hope you will find in 2 Peter and what I have written both a strong affirmation of your ministry and a challenge to grow. If you are not a teacher now, consider this book an invitation to examine the possibility that you are one of the few called to teach.

12

1 *Why Do We Do It?*

"Grow in the grace and knowledge of our Lord and Savior Jesus Christ."   *2 Peter 3:18*

In spite of James' warning, "Let not many of you become teachers" (3:1), every fall hundreds of thousands of men and women, in congregations all over the world, meet their classes to begin anew their ministry of teaching. Of all the areas of service in the church, few can enlist the time and talents of more lay people than does the church school. Though almost all these teachers are volunteers, education in the church is not free. In America alone congregations spend millions of dollars every year on materials. The costs for buildings and utilities to support educational programs must be in the billions of dollars. In terms of time, talents, energy, and dollars and cents, the church has a vast investment in its teaching ministry. With all that is invested, certainly we should think about why we teach. Of course, we teach because Jesus commanded us to teach (Matt. 28:16-20). But what is it we hope to see happen in the lives of those we teach? What do we want them to learn?

Educational goal of 2 Peter

In his opening and closing phrases the author of 2 Peter informed his readers of his hopes. He began with the prayer that "grace and peace be multiplied" among them, and concluded with the exhortation to "grow in the grace and knowledge of the Lord and Savior Jesus Christ." Growth is the central theme of 2 Peter, and for that reason it is a text especially appropriate for teachers.

Growth is a fundamental educational concept. It provides a basis for understanding students, teachers, and what they are about together. Basically, growth is a concept that recognizes the reality of change. Teaching is an attempt to give direction to change in order that its consequences be positive. In 2 Peter that direction is very clear; it is growth in the grace and knowledge of Jesus Christ. That, according to the author of the letter, is the purpose for Christian education. Before saying more about this purpose, I would like to illustrate some ways in which the principle of growth helps us to understand both teachers and students.

Growth and individual differences in students

It would be a rare class, indeed, where all the students are at the same level of development. One of the first things teachers discover about their students is that they are all different. Some are healthier than others, some read better than others, and some are liked better than others. While we know all that to be true, we don't always recognize that they also learn in different ways and grow at varying rates.

Acting on the principle of individual differences can have many implications for teachers. The first, and probably the most obvious, is that it involves more work. At the same time, it can also mean greater satisfaction for teachers as they observe their students growing in ways that are appropriate to them. More specifically, it means accepting students where they are. What a relief that can be for teachers who think that all of their students must "perform" at the same level. What a relief that could be for students who may have

14

felt judged because they weren't where they were "supposed" to be. But the relief has a price tag—work and effort on the part of the teacher. Teachers have to spend more time getting to know their students, finding out what they know and don't know, and how they seem to learn best. By accepting students with their individual differences, teachers are better able to provide learning activities that both affirm their students as persons and challenge them to grow. The latter point is critical. Without challenging students, accepting them may be an easy attempt at teacher popularity and a denial of teacher responsibility. I've experienced both.

I especially remember Ira. He was an Eskimo boy in an upper-elementary class in a village school in Alaska. Over the six years that he had been eligible to attend, Ira had missed most of his classes. As a result, he could barely do the most elementary work. Ira was also the most picked-on boy in the class. He didn't seem to have many friends. When he entered my class, I decided to befriend him. Whenever he came to class, I made a special point to welcome him. I made an effort to let him know that I cared for him. I was rewarded for my efforts with warm smiles and an attendance pattern much improved over Ira's previous years in school. Ira was affirmed in our class. In me he found a friend—someone who accepted him. That's good, but I didn't help Ira learn. Unfortunately, he left my class at about the same reading and computational skill level that he entered with. I failed to challenge him, and in that failure, Ira was not as well-equipped for living as he might have been.

Teachers cannot learn for their students. They can't make them grow. A teacher's responsibility is to assist students in their growing—growth they'll need for living in the present and for all the joys and sorrows that life will hold for them. This assistance begins when teachers ask themselves about each student: what affirms and challenges him or her to grow? Once that's determined, teachers are in a position to look for and organize the materials their students will need.

Using the teacher's guide to good advantage is one way to go about this. The alternate activities suggested there are not only to give variety to a class; they are there to help meet the needs of the variety of students who are there.

For teachers willing to invest the time, all sorts of materials are available for class and student enrichment. The task is to locate them and connect them with growing students.

All the available helps for growth won't do much good, however, unless teachers seriously acknowledge differences among their students. Finding out what those differences are and where students are in their development provides the foundation for helping them to grow through affirmation and challenge. Knowing the need and the possibilities for growth can motivate teachers to get involved enough to give that growth a chance.

Growth and individual differences in teachers

Teachers come in all sizes, shapes, and ages. They come from a variety of backgrounds. Some are just beginning, while others have been at it for decades. Like their students, not all have grown to the same maturity in their ability to teach or in their understanding of the Christian faith. It would be unrealistic—and undesirable—to want all teachers to be the same. What can be expected, however, is that teachers grow. They don't have to be the same teachers year after year. They can become more effective—better able to teach and more knowledgeable about their calling.

What allows them to grow are the same things that apply to their students: affirmation and challenge. A significant part of affirmation has to come from within the teacher. Those who don't have a sense of call, urgency, and conviction about their teaching may have an insatiable need for the affirmation of others. Even with inner conviction, most teachers need encouragement and support. It is often close at hand. Students don't always say thanks or tell you they enjoy a class, but their participation in activities often express it.

Teachers need to be aware of that and accept it as genuine—whether it comes from learners who are children, youths, or adults.

An encouraging word may also come from parents of the children and youths who are taught. In a survey conducted by a seminary class, teachers stated that one of the greatest needs in the church school was for more parental involvment. I think many parents are appreciative of those who teach their children. Teachers aren't always aware of it, however. Stopping by before or after class, an occasional card, or even an invitation for dessert or dinner could go a long way to affirm teachers in their ministry.

Other teachers, members of boards of parish education, and pastors have a special responsibility to affirm those who teach. This support can't be given, of course, unless it is known who is teaching, where they teach, and what is happening in the church school. Again, this takes time, involvement, and presence. Those congregations interested in the growth of their teachers will make the necessary investment.

Challenge, too, is a part of a teacher's growing. The shape of the challenge depends a great deal on the strengths and needs of both teachers and their students. In-service training sessions are one way to help. Workshops and meetings, however, have little interest or effect unless teachers see themselves as ones who, like their students, are engaged in a continuous pilgrimage. This leads to another, closely related idea about growing: neither students nor their teachers ever arrive.

The continuing aspect of growth

One of the most difficult persons for me to work with is the one who communicates in some way: "You can't teach me anything." I realize this is, in part, my problem—an area of growth for me. It's also a problem for the other. What it seems to say is that the person thinks that he or she has arrived and has nothing more to learn. Such persons tend to be defensive, closed, argumentative, judgmental—and afraid. All are traits of those who seem to sense no need to grow in themselves and see no possibilities for it in others. What an unfortunate perspective to have! Not only does it put an unnecessary lid on the person's life, but it puts others into boxes where they don't belong. Its results often are prejudice and exploitation.

The marvelous thing about God's acts for us is that God has already made us all we could ever become. Yet in this life we will never attain to all we could be—no matter how much we grow. In Christ, God has redeemed us. By grace God has made us new, free to be children of God. Becoming a child of God is through birth, or rebirth. Birth is always beyond the power of the one being born. It comes through the life of another, whether from a physical parent or through the Holy Spirit. In Baptism the gift of life is given. There is nothing to be demonstrated, nothing to learn in order to become God's child.

Being born the children of God, however, we are called to grow to maturity (Col. 1:28). For the apostle Paul, reaching maturity had nothing to do with attaining a certain place or position. With maturity comes the realization that our lives in Christ are dynamic. We never arrive. The Christian life is characterized by the movement and growth that holds out ever richer and more profound possibilities for living in Christ Jesus. Paul described this dynamic nature in Phil. 3:12-15:

Not that I have already obtained this or am already perfect; but I press on to make it my own, because Christ Jesus has made me his own. Brethren, I do not consider that I have made it my own; but one thing I do, forgetting what lies behind and straining forward to what lies ahead, I press on toward the goal for the prize of the upward call of God in Christ Jesus. Let those of us who are mature be thus minded.

The idea of growing, of the Christian life as dynamic, is one of the most exciting and powerful dimensions of Christian education. The Christian faith is not only what God has done in the past. It is a matter of the present and future as well. It assumes there is a

18

future, and the future belongs to God. We are called to identify with it, be a part of it, strive for it, hope for it, pray for it—that God's kingdom will come to us and to all humankind.

Growth and competition

The concept of growth is also freeing in that it puts competition in a proper perspective. Competition can be destructive if the participants view their striving only in terms of being against each other, when they find their value in how they compare with each other. Such comparisons, I suppose, can't be avoided. But as Christians, our concern is with God's kingdom and with what God is calling us to be and do. There is no one to surpass, no one to put down. Our worth need not be proved; it is already ours.

One evening my wife and I took a bike ride. On our way home we saw our elderly neighbor, who is recovering from a stroke. With the aid of his walker, he was making his way down the alley, as he does several times a day. It's a slow process, but he stays at it day after day. He's not in competition with anyone. He simply wants to walk and to be about the best he can. He is striving to grow.

Teachers and students in Christian education don't have to compete either. Competition has the potential for unfair comparisons and disappointment. We don't all have to have the same spiritual experience, the same vocabulary, the same style, the same answers to all of life's questions in order to be "in the race." We do have the same Lord. Jesus invites us to grow in his grace, and often his grace allows both students and teachers to attain heights they would never have imagined if they had been competing with another person.

One remarkable woman who has come a long way on the journey on which God is leading her is Mother Teresa of Calcutta. Her journey has brought her into contact with the poor and outcast of the world. It has also brought her acclaim and admiration. Could she have imagined that ministry if she had seen her life only in

19

competition with others? Could she have accomplished so much if at some earlier point in her life she had decided that she had arrived? Can we know where God is leading us? To some extent, perhaps, but there is a special excitement and mystery in seeing life as a journey. It's an enthusiasm that is apprehended and realized in faith—trust that God holds us and leads us into the future.

Christian teachers have a part in all of this. Their openness to where God is leading them serves as a powerful invitation to others to embark on, or continue, their journeys of faith. In the classroom the faith journeys of others can be explored and alternatives considered for where God is leading now. Teachers must help their students to see the Christian life as more than routine and obligation. God intended it to be an exciting journey—not always pleasant or fun, but a life that, nevertheless, is going somewhere. In such a life there is no room for the sense of having arrived. That's deadly for students, teachers, and the church. God always has more to give, and we have more to grow.

I could never exhaust all that could be written about growth. Before leaving the subject, however, let me suggest some questions to help you reflect on your growing.

What is your attitude toward growing?

Is the word *dynamic* descriptive of your life and faith? What are your strengths that could be developed further?

What are problem areas in your teaching and in your congregation's educational program?

Where is the mission of the church leading you?

Think about ways you can grow. Allow yourself to be challenged. Don't be afraid of taking some risks.

At the same time, are you affirming and challenging your students?

What kinds of expectations do you have of them?

What are you striving to accomplish in your relationship with them?

Try responding to the following exercise. Check which category best fits you. What do your responses say about your attitude and expectations for growth?

I think of my calling as a teacher as:
- [ ] a ministry to people
- [ ] going somewhere
- [ ] reaching out
- [ ] taking risks
- [ ] future oriented
- [ ] having a vision
- [ ] what it can become
- [ ] a job to be done
- [ ] always about the same
- [ ] hanging on
- [ ] defensive and protective
- [ ] past oriented
- [ ] focused on a memory
- [ ] what it is or was

Growing in grace and knowledge

Students and teachers are to be growing together *in the grace and knowledge of our Lord Jesus Christ. Grace* is defined as the unmerited love of God for us. God has done all that can be done in making us his children. In love God has chosen us, redeemed us in Christ, and raised us to newness of life.

Because grace is God's gift to give, teachers have no control over it. They can, however, be instruments of God's grace as they teach God's Word and assist others to realize the grace of God in their lives. In doing so, teachers might well keep several things in mind. First, growth in grace has no limitations in terms of time or space. Grace may be experienced more significantly in settings unrelated to instruction than in any classroom situation. A friend of mine, a psychiatrist, wonders if any growth can occur except through trial and struggle, as Christians are confronted by the sorrows and joys of living. If that's true, significant moments for growth are going to come in homes, in schools, and in workplaces—wherever people are deeply affected by what is transpiring in their lives. There they will experience the strong hand of God upholding them. There they will sense the affirming presence of God and respond to the challenge of living as God's people.

Because this is true, Christian teachers need to know something of the world from which their students come. For the teacher, visits to homes, schools, offices, factories, and places of business are important extensions of what goes on in the classroom. I know one lay catechist who seldom misses a play, a concert, or an athletic event at her local junior and senior high school. She talks about what she hears and sees with the confirmands when they come to church on Wednesday evenings. It helps to establish a sound relationship between herself and her students.

Students will also be served by teachers who have developed skills in listening. As people live out their lives, questions and doubts arise. Sometimes they are the doubts of others. Once they've been raised they don't go away. Perhaps questions surface from something a teacher has said in school or something that's been heard on TV. There is much to cause both youth and adults to wonder about what they believe. Allowing these questions to be raised in class provides a structure in which to discuss life experiences in the context of the confession of faith. Listening will not only allow for the surfacing of doubts, it can also lead to discoveries of the students' other personal needs that arise out of their life situations. The time we have with them in class is short, but if we listen in order to hear their hurts, opportunities will come to share the love of God and the grace of our Lord Jesus Christ.

Nevertheless, with the limited amount of time teachers have and with the realization of the impact life experience has on what is believed and done, teachers may sometimes wonder about the value of what they do. Does it really make any difference?

That question struck home for me not long ago while I was driving on the freeway. I was passed by a police car that was apparently responding to an accident. A few moments later an ambulance passed with its red lights flashing. My first reaction was to pray for the persons who were likely in desperate need of help. Then my thoughts turned to those who were rushing to meet their need. *There,* I thought, *are people who are really useful. The police, the medics, the medical doctors who would be there to give aid, and in that service, could give a witness to Jesus Christ.* And what was I? I was a teacher on his way to class. Oh, I like to think that some exciting things happen in my classes, but how can that be compared with ministry in a crisis situation?

Then I remembered a phone call my wife and I had received some months earlier from friends in a congregation we had served in California. They told us of a young woman, Joleen, who had been on her way to a weekend of skiing. She apparently had fallen asleep and driven off a mountain road and crashed against some trees. She died within hours of the accident. But before she died, she had the opportunity to confess her faith. Someone had stopped at the scene of the accident, found our young friend, and talked to her about Jesus. What she said to Joleen was not new. Joleen recalled what she had been taught by loving parents and teachers throughout her life—and in that knowledge she died. Nothing could have given greater comfort to her parents who mourned her.

People in crisis situations do have special opportunities to minister. But as I think about it, much of what they are able to do depends on what those people in need know and believe at the point of the crisis. What they know depends on what they have been taught by parents, or in a class somewhere by a teacher who helped to provide a foundation for all of life's experiences, whatever they might be.

The classroom is also a place where the grace of God is experienced. Teachers are witnesses to it in many ways. God's grace is there when students exercise the marvelous gift of forgiveness for each other and their teacher. It's there when someone says: "It's really true, isn't it—this love of God for us. I believe it." We know that's a miracle only God performs.

Students can experience grace in a classroom. It may come in a relationship with a teacher or friend who truly loves them for the sake of Jesus. It may come in the singing of a song, the quiet of a prayer, the touch of another's hand. The list of ways could go on and on—but above all, for both students and teachers, grace comes in knowledge. In the study of the Bible both young and old can learn more about God, who reveals himself there.

We refer to the Bible as a means of grace. Through it, and in it, God reveals his gracious will for us and all humankind. As we teach, study, and learn, opening ourselves to what God has to give, we are enlightened by the Holy Spirit. In the Scriptures we are constantly affirmed in who we are and challenged to participate in the work of God's kingdom.

As we teach and learn God's Word, we also discover people who are not unlike ourselves. The Bible does not whitewash human nature. It shows us people who struggled with self-righteousness and vanity, just as people do today. They came face to face with dying, despair, and disillusionment. They felt anger over God's seeming rejection and elation over God's deliverance. This human drama is lived out against the background of a gracious God who loved the unlovable so much that he gave his only Son to die that they could be redeemed.

To grow in grace is to become increasingly aware of this great love with which God has loved us. One of the first Bible verses learned in church school is John 3:16: "For God so loved the world that he gave his only Son." The first song is often "Jesus Loves Me." We learn them so early in life we may be tempted to think that we came into the world knowing them or that we learned them out of our experience. That is not the case. We could never have known the love of God unless God had chosen to show it to us—especially in Jesus Christ. This is the revelation of the Scriptures. It's the story

Christian teachers first receive for themselves—and the story they are called to teach to others.

Through teaching and learning the story and connecting it with the varied experiences, hopes, and dreams of life, Christians grow in grace and knowledge. In his commentary on 2 Peter, Michael Green wrote: "Knowledge of Christ and knowledge about Christ are, if they keep pace with one another, both the safeguard against heresy and apostasy and also the means of growth in grace. For the more we know Christ, the more we will invoke his grace. And the more we know about Christ, the more varied will be the grace we invoke." [1] In the next chapter we will consider the particular knowledge that the author of 2 Peter commended for growing in grace.

2 *Knowledge Worth Knowing*

"Grow in the grace and knowledge of our Lord and Savior Jesus Christ."   2 Peter 3:18

Over 100 years ago Herbert Spencer wrote a short book that has had a profound effect on education. He entitled it *What Knowledge Is of Most Worth?* He argued that his question could be answered only against the background of a prior one: What is the purpose for education? For Spencer, the purpose was complete life. The knowledge of greatest worth was that which contributed the most to the realization of the complete life. While there have been many who have disagreed with Spencer's objective or his definition of the complete life, few today would disagree with his premise: content serves purpose.

According to 2 Peter, the purpose of Christian education is growth in the grace and knowledge of our Lord Jesus Christ. Starting there, we could ask ourselves: of all the information we *could* teach, what has the greatest worth in terms of Peter's purpose? It's an important question. The amount of material from which to choose is staggering. Within the Bible alone there is enough to occupy the better part of a person's life in teaching and learning. The gospel of John concludes with the thought that the entire world could not contain all the books that would have been necessary to tell everything Jesus had said and done (John 21:25). Libraries, bookstores, and book catalogs seem to reveal an effort at accomplishing what wasn't done in the first century—filling the world with books. Out of all the available information, what has the greatest worth in helping teachers and students to grow in Jesus Christ?

Writers and editors of resource materials for Christian education have done much to make that decision. In the introductions to most teacher's guides are statements about the purpose of the material to be taught. These statements are theological and reflect the beliefs of the writers and editors. It's assumed that the biblical stories and activities used in the materials support those purposes. Before endorsing any published materials, those responsible for educational programs should be thoroughly familiar with their purpose and content and whether they reflect the theology of the congregation.

Teachers, however, are not called to put into practice only the ideas and plans of others. They, too, are responsible for thinking about the purpose of their teaching and how the concepts they are teaching help to achieve those purposes. In the first classes I taught I wasn't too concerned with an overall purpose. I was hoping to get through the hour. That's probably normal for the beginning teacher. As teachers mature, however, they become aware of the larger scope of what they are doing. They realize that they can neither teach everything there is to know, nor can they teach the same lesson in every class. Teachers are a part of a team, linked together in a common purpose. Getting beyond survival and joining in this common purpose is part of the excitement of teaching. At this point teachers join the theologians of the church in asking: what is it that God would have us believe and do? What is the mission of the church? What knowledge is worth knowing?

If my experience in the church school is typical, teachers and parents are concerned about curriculum materials. Teachers often discuss what they think is best. That's a necessary discussion. My hope is that it goes beyond colors, costs, the number of activities, and teacher helps. All of these are important, but only as they relate to the intended purpose of the teacher. The writer of 2 Peter was concerned about growing in the grace and knowledge of our Lord Jesus Christ. There is a close relationship between grace and knowledge. As we come to know more about Jesus and to know Jesus more, we grow in his grace. The content that we teach, the knowledge we have students learn, *is* very significant.

Though the letter is brief, the author of 2 Peter gives several strong indications as to what he believed was the knowledge of greatest worth in Christian growing. The first is knowledge of the identity of God and of those who are God's children. The second is knowledge about how to live a fruitful Christian life. And third is the knowledge that there are false teachers who seek to destroy faith and discipleship. As you read the following, and the second epistle of Peter, compare it with what you believe, teach, and hope for in your students. What is your purpose for teaching? What is— for you—the knowledge of greatest worth?

The knowledge of the identity of God and of God's people

For the author of 2 Peter, knowledge of and about God is of the greatest value. To know God is to know God as triune. The author of 2 Peter didn't try to explain the Trinity. He simply acknowledged that he knows God as Father, Son, and Holy Spirit. The Father is the creator of the heavens and the earth (2 Peter 3:5). He is the Father of the Lord Jesus Christ, and on the Mount of Transfiguration he affirmed the identity and ministry of Jesus (2 Peter 1:17). The Father is patient and merciful, even more than many would have him be. He graciously waits for people to repent (2 Peter 3:9). The Father is beyond all limitations of time, yet uses time to carry out his will (3:8-9). If the Father is merciful, he is also wrathful to those who mock him (2:4-10; 3:7).

Jesus is the beloved Son of God, the one in whom the Father is well pleased (1:17). Jesus is the Christ, the fulfillment of God's promise to send a Savior (1:1-2). And Jesus is Lord, the one who is worthy of obedience, worship, and service (1:11; 3:18). Christians today commonly use the phrase "Lord and Savior Jesus Christ." It's a beautiful phrase that summarizes in a few words who Jesus is. The author of 2 Peter is the only one of the New Testament writers to use it.

The coming again of Jesus in power is of most importance in 2 Peter. This future orientation is in contrast to the comparatively small place given to the events of Jesus' life. For example, there is nothing in 2 Peter directly about either the crucifixion or the resurrection. The one event in the life of Jesus to which the writer does allude is the transfiguration. His strong affirmation of Jesus' return in power is dependent, however, on his belief in his resurrection and ascension. The ascended Lord, he wrote, will come like a thief in the night (3:10). When he comes, he will destroy the old world and put in its place "new heavens and a new earth in which righteousness dwells" (3:13). This emphasis upon the future indicates that for Peter faith was as much a trust of what God will do as what God has done. To be Christian is to confess not only that God was in Christ, but that God is working out his purposes among us today, and that one day Christ will come in power. In 2 Peter the thrust most definitely is forward, and that is consistent with the purpose of growth.

The Holy Spirit is the source of inspiration. Through the Holy Spirit the prophets received the messages they were to deliver to God's people. While the Spirit works through individual persons, the Spirit also inspires the church. Specifically, when prophecy is to be interpreted, it is to be done in the context of the community of believers, which, in turn, is inspired by the Holy Spirit (2 Peter 1:19-21).

Arising out of all of this we can say the following about the identity of God as revealed in 2 Peter. God is purposeful—as creator, redeemer, and inspirer. God's purpose is, to borrow a phrase from Paul, to bring humankind to the realization that in Christ all have been reconciled to God (2 Cor. 5:19). God is also active. Through his own initiative God has acted and continues to act to accomplish his purpose. God is also a God of promise. He has promised that Christ will come again in power—to take unto himself the redeemed. In the purpose, activity, and promise of God, his people are daily affirmed and invited to participate in the mission God has for his world.

To know God is one side of the identity question. The other, for the writer of 2 Peter, is the identity of his readers. Who are they? 2 Peter portrays them as having two identities. On the one hand, they are referred to as "those who have obtained a faith of equal standing with ours in the righteousness of our God and Savior Jesus Christ" (2 Peter 1:1). These are the ones for whom Christ had died—the ones he had saved from corruption and made to be the children of God.

Yet the author of 2 Peter saw his readers as ones who had not utterly escaped the limitations of the flesh. They continued to be susceptible to their passions, and they were always potential targets for exploitation by false teachers. They were continually confronted by challenges to their faith. Doubt was very real to them. They were people torn between two worlds. In faith they had confessed Jesus as their Lord and Savior. Still, they were people who could remember their close identification with passion and self-pride. Only by remaining and growing in the grace of God could their identity as God's children be assured (2 Peter 1:10). They were both saints and sinners, and so are we.

It would be almost impossible to overemphasize the value of this knowledge for teachers. In it the teacher is challenged to take the risks that can lead to exciting moments of learning. At the same time, it helps us to realize that failure and disappointments are always possibilities—because we and those we teach are sinners. Remembering that we are at the same time saints and sinners helps us to accept that no class, no learning, no relationship is perfect. It also assures us that in every situation there is the grace of God to bless, make whole, and grant understanding.

Knowledge and the fruitful life

Knowing that God loves us so much that he gave his only Son to die for us and that through Jesus we have been made the children of God is to have knowledge of the greatest worth. In it we are affirmed in who we are, assured in the hope of salvation, and set free to live our lives in obedience to the one who has called us out of darkness into his marvelous light (1 Peter 2:9). How is it, then, that the faithful are to live? One response is that we have been called to live a fruitful life.

For at least two reasons teachers may be hesitant to deal with the subject of the fruitful life. First, there is the fear of work righteousness. In *Freedom for Ministry* Richard John Neuhaus maintained that because of that fear many would drive a wedge between faith and behavior. He wrote:

> Many Christians today, unfortunately, are made very nervous by the idea of the worthy or good life. The idea of the good life smacks too much of pagan classicism or of the smug self-righteousness that Jesus condemned in some of his contemporaries.[1]

Teachers in the church *are* in danger of falling into the trap of works righteousness and moralism. There are those who insist that salvation is based on justice and not mercy. They argue that one has to earn salvation. This is contrary to the gospel. Salvation is by grace through faith. It is a gift of God, lest anyone should boast (Eph. 2:8-9). There is also, however, the danger of separating faith and life as though there were no relationship between them. If fear of works righteousness has gone that far, it has gone too far. Neuhaus went on to say that even if theologians attempt such a separation, the people of the church will not allow it.

32

If they cannot count on the church for some kind of binding or normative ethic, and if the Christian faith does not help tie together the disparate pieces of a confused universe, they will begin to wonder what is the point of it all.[2]

The inherent sense of connectedness between faith and life is portrayed consistently throughout the New Testament. Jesus said in Matt. 7:20: "Thus you will know them by their fruits." Ephesians 5 begins with the exhortation, "Be imitators of God." The writer then enumerates several qualities identified with such an imitation. Paul, the theologian of justification by faith, commended the following as the fruit of the Spirit: "love, joy, peace, patience, kindness, goodness, faithfulness, gentleness, self-control" (Gal. 5:22). These passages certainly show that knowledge of a fruitful life is of considerable value.

A second reason why teachers may hesitate to deal with the fruitful life is that there is considerable confusion as to what it is. Just how is it that Christians are to live, and what is the basis for saying so? The church cannot escape the fact that it lives within a culture. By and large, Western culture today is extremely reluctant to commend any particular behavior as any better or worse than another. We live in an era of individualism with respect to ethics. Two phrases seem to point to that individualism: "If it feels good, do it," and "It all depends on where you're coming from." Since not all feel good about the same thing, or come from the same place, it would seem that there is no behavior that is any more commendable than any other. If that is the case, how can one teach about the fruitful life with any specificity? From that point of view the only knowledge that has worth is values clarification. According to that approach, what is important about values is not what they are, but knowing how to arrive at them.

Is the fruitful *Christian* life only a matter of how one feels or where a person is coming from? Are attitudes about marriage, family, abortion, honesty, work, justice, nuclear power, and worship

33

only a matter of each person's viewpoint? Of course, finally each person comes to his or her own conclusions. Outside of mind-control techniques, teachers can't make value decisions for their students. Nevertheless, that does not preclude the possibility, and the necessity, that the church—and most especially its teachers—search for common ground with respect to the fruitful life. The teachings of Jesus, Paul, and 2 Peter affirm that such common ground exists. The actual words and phrases used to describe the ground vary, but the essential nature to which they point is remarkably similar. 2 Peter describes the fruitful life in the following:

> For this very reason make every effort to supplement your faith with virtue, and virtue with knowledge, and knowledge with self-control, and self-control with steadfastness, and steadfastness with godliness, and godliness with brotherly affection, and brotherly affection with love (1:5-7).

One of the characteristics of these qualities is their open-endedness. This provides the Christian with both freedom and responsibility. There is the freedom to inquire what it means to be loving or patient in any given situation. This is not a set of rules that simply calls for implementation. If it were, all teachers would have to do is teach the rules and insist on compliance. The same behavior would be expected of all—with no room for either creativity or growth. There may be some who would prefer it that way, but it is not the freedom of the gospel.

On the other hand, Christians have the responsibility of particularizing these qualities in given situations. It is not enough to affirm the value of self-control in general. Certainly it is not enough to list it in response to a question on a Bible quiz. Self-control, along with other qualities, is meant to be worked out in the life situations where Christians find themselves. Not all Christians will do this in the same way. Christians are growing persons, and challenge is a part of that growing. Challenges set before small children are not the same as those that confront adults. Every person must be challenged to grow and to bear fruit as they have been enabled by the Holy Spirit. This idea is essential in protecting the concern for the fruitful life from degenerating into legalism.

Legalism sets one pattern of behaving as the norm for all. In so doing, it tends to support some people and judge others. Taken seriously, it leads to absolute despair because no one can live up to the demands of the law (Rom. 7:19-25). The gospel leaves no room for this legalism. From it, whether imposed by others or ourselves, Christ has set us free.

The activity of Ruth Youngdahl Nelson is an example of that freedom. She is a mother, grandmother, church leader, and writer of considerable renown. In the summer of 1982 she acted on her convictions about nuclear warfare. She joined her son and others who attempted to block the passage of a submarine equipped to carry nuclear weapons. Along with several others, she was arrested for her protest.

A legalistic outlook might insist that Ruth Nelson's behavior is the norm for all Christians. Or, it could as likely condemn her for acting in what some might call an un-Christian manner. Either would be a mistaken understanding of our freedom in the gospel and our capacity for growth. Five years ago Ruth Nelson may not have acted in this way. In the future she may find other ways to express her concern for God's creation. But for now, she is expressing herself as a free and responsible person — attempting to live a fruitful Christian life.

Christian teachers are about the task of assisting others to understand and act on the freedom and responsibility they have in Jesus Christ. Understanding and doing are dynamic and growing. We have different expectations of children than we have of adults—and even different expectations of those who are the same age. All are persons who are called to grow in their own personal and mysterious ways. Nevertheless, the fruitful life has a common origin. It is built on the solid foundation of Jesus Christ; there is no other (1 Cor. 3:11). And, however imperfectly, the fruitful life reflects

Christ's image and the qualities commended to us in the apostolic tradition. For those who would live such a life, this is knowledge of great worth.

Knowledge of false teachers

The threat of false teachers is a persistent theme throughout the Scriptures. Two conditions bring about this threat. One of them is a truth claim. Without a truth claim there would be no standard for making judgments. A second condition is a challenge to the truth—either by another claim or the denial that there is such a thing as truth. Seldom, if ever, have these conditions been lacking. They were there in the first century of the church's life, and as long as the church continues to affirm the gospel as true, it can expect to struggle with the issue of true and false teachers.

How the struggle is waged is often dependent on each side's perception of where their strength lies. The early church had no political power. It affirmed truth through preaching and teaching. One is reminded of the words of Paul: "For I am not ashamed of the gospel; it is the power of God for salvation to every one who has faith, to the Jew first and also to the Greek" (Rom. 1:16). Those who opposed the church often resorted to violence through the exercise of political power. Once the church gained some of the same power, it tended to adopt the same policy toward those thought to be false teachers.

The second letter of Peter reflects a time when the church was without political power. The church's strength was in what it taught and preached—Jesus Christ. If the church was to be strong, then its teachers had to be strong. Their strength was in their confession of Jesus Christ as Savior, their submission to him as Lord, and their hope in him as the one who was coming again in power. To deny any of these three, or to encourage others to do the same, was to be a false teacher.

The writer of 2 Peter was a realist. He had no illusions about the world or the human condition. He recognized the human craving

36

for self-worth, and knew that all attempts short of repentance would fail in realizing it (2 Peter 3:9). He was aware of challenges to the gospel, both from within the church and from without. He had heard the claims of those who insisted that the good life consisted in following one's own passions, and not the Lord Jesus. He also knew that while only a few might dare to make those claims publicly, there were many who were only waiting to hear them and use them as a justification for their own behavior. Unable to see where they were being led, they were more than willing to be exploited by those who taught them (2 Peter 2:3).

Jesus told his disciples that before they entered into discipleship they should count the cost (Luke 14:33). That cost, said Jesus, was the giving of their very lives. A part of this cost is identifying the false claims of the world, which can seem to be so terribly attractive. Unless they are recognized for what they are, they can surprise the believer and be a cause of stumbling. The author of 2 Peter didn't want that to happen. He felt a deep need to equip the people of God to live in the world by identifying false teachers and the consequences of what they taught. For those who are going to live in the world and hope to have some impact on it, this knowledge is of great worth.

3 Faith and the Pursuit of Excellence

". . . supplement your faith with virtue."   *2 Peter 1:5*

Each vocation seems to have its own particular issues and questions that never seem to be put to rest. One of the persistent issues for education is: are teachers born or made? What do you think? Are you a teacher born or made? Does it make any difference to you?

Are teachers born or made?

Those taking the position that teachers are born tend to see teaching as an art. Artists are people who have been especially gifted in ways that allow them to write, paint, compose, or perform as others cannot. Teachers, it is argued, are much the same. In some unpredictable fashion they are able to captivate, communicate, and motivate others to learn. These qualities don't seem to be learned, and therefore persons either have them or they don't. Those who do are "born teachers."

As lofty and beautiful as this view of teaching is, it poses some problems. For example, it can make of teaching a greater mystery than it is, a riddle only those born to it can fathom. Those sensing that they lack a certain mystique may either feel intimidated or excused from trying their hand at teaching. At the other end of the spectrum, too great an emphasis on the teacher born may lead to the conclusion that teaching is easier than it is. Teaching isn't easy. It can be terribly hard work—even for gifted persons. A pianist who performs in concert may do so with no apparent effort. Before the concert, however, there are hours and hours of study and practice. If teachers are artists, they are like most of them who struggle and work at what they do and create. A teaching style doesn't just happen. A variety of skills are developed only through practice. The ability to organize learning activities comes with experience. These things all look easy for the accomplished teacher, but behind the classroom performance there is a great deal of hard work.

Not all are willing to make the effort. I recall a lesson plan submitted by a seminary student. At the bottom of the page he had written something like the following: "If teaching takes this much time and work, no wonder pastors don't want to do it." Gifted persons, thinking they can get by without working at it, may be tempted to try. Busy persons who feel they haven't time to prepare are especially susceptible to the temptation. Being a born teacher, one can probably pull it off with some regularity—but not, I think, without compromising both teaching and learning.

Those who claim that teachers are "made" usually view teaching as a *science*. Teaching and learning, they say, are governed by principles discovered by research. Teachers need to know those principles and use them as a basis for their classroom behavior. Teaching also requires certain skills, just as every profession does. Becoming a teacher means developing these skills to the degree that they can be used effectively to help others learn. Since principles and skills are learned, proponents of this view insist that teachers are made, not born.

Taken by itself, this position, too, has its problems. One is the tendency to view teaching in rather mechanical terms, as though teacher and student behavior are equal sides of an equation. Knowing principles of learning and having teacher skills can be beneficial to the teacher, but nothing guarantees that students will learn. In addition, this outlook can lead to the conviction that anyone can teach; all that is needed is for persons to be fashioned and molded into teachers. It is probably true that God has been far more generous with his gifts for teaching than many are willing to admit. However, to argue that *all* could or should teach is to invite some people to experience disaster. Like it or not, there are some who are gifted for teaching, and others who are not. According to Eph. 4:11-16, that's predictable. There are many essential ministries in the church. Each member is to find one. If it's teaching—great. If not, that's great, too.

The source of the fruitful life

By this time, you have probably concluded that teachers are both born and made. For the writer of 2 Peter, this is especially true of Christian teachers. It is his conviction that teachers, of all people, are called to live fruitful lives. This life begins in faith (2 Peter 1:5). There is no other place that it could begin. Only by faith do teachers know they are the chosen ones of God, born of the Spirit, made to be God's children. By faith alone can teachers confess Jesus Christ as Lord and Savior of the world. In faith they have their calling as teachers, trusting in God's grace to be and receive a blessing. If being born a teacher means that all these come through God's grace and nothing else, then surely the Christian teacher is born.

2 Peter goes on to commend several qualities that lead to a fruitful life:

For this very reason make every effort to supplement your faith with virtue, and virtue with knowledge, and knowledge with self-control, and self-control with steadfastness, and steadfastness with godliness, and godliness with brotherly affection, and brotherly affection with love (2 Peter 1:5-7).

Insofar as teachers grow in these qualities and allow the Holy Spirit to make their lives fruitful, it can also be said that teachers are made. In this and the following chapters attention will be given to how these qualities may assist teachers in being fruitful. As these qualities are discussed, however, it must be remembered that in both the birthing and the making of teachers, it is God's grace that equips them with everything good, in order that they may do God's will (Heb. 13:21).

A fruitful life is characterized by virtue

A fruitful life is one that is in God's will, a life pleasing to him. To do God's will is to grow in the grace and knowledge of the Lord Jesus Christ. This pleases God. Teachers are fruitful, then, as they grow and assist others in their growing. This is their particular calling. They are enriched in their vocation when they "make every effort to supplement . . . faith with virtue" (2 Peter 1:5).

Virtue is a Greek term that is something of a stranger in the New Testament. Unqualified by the gospel, the word implies that human beings are able, on their own, to fashion a life that is worthy and good. Perhaps because virtue had this connotation in the first century, it was, for the most part, avoided by early Christian writers. The author of 2 Peter made it clear, however, that virtue is not the way of salvation. Virtue refers to a quality of life in which those who are born in Christ grow to greater fruitfulness. In general it means *the active pursuit of excellence in all of life.* What we're concerned for here is teachers and their pursuit of excellence—for themselves and their students.

The quality of virtue suggests that teachers are to strive to become the best teachers they can be. This striving is done in the spirit of Christian growth. That means it is not competitive. Teachers are to strive to become the best teachers they can be with the gifts and opportunities available to them. And, virtue is an active,

42

dynamic quality. Teachers never reach *the* point of excellence. Whether they have taught for five or 20 years, teachers can expect to grow in their skills and understanding, but they'll never arrive. Experience will only give greater meaning and direction to the pursuit of excellence.

The challenge to pursue excellence in teaching is more than pious rhetoric. After all, God hasn't saved us for the sake of mediocrity. God calls us to be all we can be by the grace that he has given. What's more, this challenge is as much for our sake as it is for God's. If God is pleased by those who do his will, those doing God's will are pleased if they do it well. People enjoy what they do well. What they enjoy, they tend to give their time to—enlarging their knowledge and developing their skills.

On the other hand, there is resistance to those activities that result in failure or disappointment. This can keep us from trying new activities. Unsure of our ability to do them well, we have a tendency to stay with the tested and true. The willingness to take risks with the new is dependent on previous growth and the setting in which the risk is taken. The measure of risk must not be so great that it overwhelms the possibilities for growth.

Those responsible for helping teachers in their pursuit of excellence might well keep this in mind. New concepts, materials, and skills will more likely be appreciated if they are introduced and practiced by teachers in a safe setting than if their use is expected to just happen under the pressure of the classroom.

Excellence: a source of joy

I hope that all teachers in the church find joy in their teaching, though no one should expect every moment to be marvelous. The overall result, however, should be one of satisfaction. The more that's true, the less difficult it will be to recruit and keep teachers in the church school.

A few years ago a young man I know started to teach Sunday school. It didn't go particularly well, but he stayed with it, and he grew in his ability to work with young people. Now his students follow him around, convinced they are fortunate to have him for their teacher. Not long ago he was considering transferring to another city. Among the considerations involved in his decision to stay was his Sunday school class.

Those who want to teach, and continue teaching, are those who have a sense of doing well. They are also the ones who are most likely to want to become even better teachers. (A survey of Sunday school teachers found that those who spent an hour or more preparing for their classes were far more interested in attending inservice training sessions than were those who spent 15 minutes or less in preparation.) All of this is directly related to the quality of *virtue*—the pursuit of excellence to be the best teacher one can be.

The pursuit of excellence: a source of motivation

When the pursuit of excellence characterizes a church school or a whole congregation, exciting things happen. It's not just a matter of business as usual. Sunday school is more than the hour between services or the place where children are left by their parents or where some adults do their duty for God. The pursuit of excellence stimulates people to think and to act creatively. This brings new ideas, new enthusiasm, new possibilities, and new excitement. Of course, it also means work and effort, but what a great environment in which to teach and learn!

In his research on American congregations, Lyle Schaller found many that fit his definition of the "passive church." These congregations are particularly lacking in virtue—the pursuit of excellence. He found a high degree of passivity in congregations where:

(a) there is a lack of a consistent and continuing emphasis on opportunities for personal and spiritual growth for adults, (b) there is a comparatively low level of competence in the members, and especially the leaders, in articulating their faith, (this characteristic often is reinforced by the lack of any programmatic emphasis to help people develop this ability).[1]

There are, wrote Schaller, four characteristics of the passive congregation:

1. Passivity replaces enthusiasm.
2. Divisiveness replaces a sense of unity.
3. "Goal-lessness" replaces an emphasis upon specific goals.
4. Drift replaces a sense of direction.[2]

Although there are many causes for a congregation to slip into passivity, two are most common, according to Schaller. The first is a growing emphasis on institutional self-preservation as over against a mission of outreach. This is reflected in a low priority on evangelism, education, nurture, and involvement in community ministries. "Another common cause of passivity is the orientation toward today and tomorrow gradually being replaced with an increasingly strong orientation to the past."[3]

There are, undoubtedly, some who prefer the passive to the growing church. It makes few if any demands. Absent is a sense of struggle with what God is moving the congregation to do and how it is to be done. Changing such a situation may be very difficult. It's not likely that it can happen all at once. Schaller recommends that it begin with a redefinition of the role and identity of the congregation.[4] The definition of the church in 2 Peter as a people growing in the grace and knowledge of the Lord Jesus Christ, engaged in the pursuit of excellence, may just be the place where this redefinition could begin.

In any case, whether a church is dynamic or passive, what might characterize the pursuit of excellence in teaching? If there is anything that calls for creativity on the part of teachers and those responsible for education in a congregation, it's precisely this question. Just to get things started, let me make a few suggestions.

To begin the pursuit of excellence in teaching

One place to start is at the point where teachers are selected and invited to teach. If teachers are recruited out of desperation, without thought about the gifts they could bring to teaching, their preparation, and the needs of students, the church school already has problems. As often as not, desperation leads the recruiter to tell the prospective teacher: "Don't worry about how to do it. Anyone can teach. There's nothing to it." That's an expression of absolute confidence in the notion that teachers are made. Unfortunately, when desperation is the rule, once candidates have said yes to teaching, they are often assumed to be born teachers. It's not uncommon for them to be given a list of names and a pile of materials, shown a place to teach, invited to attend an orientation session—and then left on their own.

To be fair, what else can be done when a candidate says yes in late August and Sunday school begins the second week in September? I am also aware that volunteers for the church school aren't all that easy to find. And even when teachers are recruited in this way, many do have an extremely rich ministry. The approach, however, doesn't reflect much concern for the pursuit of excellence.

We need to be honest. Teaching isn't easy—not if it is to be done well. That's why one of the most important responsibilities of a congregation's education committee is selecting and preparing teachers for their calling. What's involved is looking for those who seem to be born teachers—and equipping them. The process used in selecting them is not of greatest importance, but the more the process is removed from the state of desperation, the more effective it is likely to be. A suggested approach is described in Appendix A.

Once teachers are selected, they deserve to be equipped for teaching. This would include an orientation to the congregation's educational program—how it is organized and what its purposes are. All teachers will benefit from knowing where they fit into the overall program. Those who haven't taught before could be expected to attend a teacher-training course. Many published materials for such a course are available. One that I recommend is *I Want to be a Teacher* by Eugene Kreider (Augsburg, 1981). During, and at the end of the course, participants should have some options.

46

One is that they not teach. It may be easier to get people to attend the teacher-training course if they know they will not necessarily have to teach. Other options could include serving as an aid, further observing of other teachers, team teaching, or taking a class. These options may seem a bit luxurious, especially if there is a desperate need for teachers. If the selection and training of teachers is done well in advance of anticipated needs, the options could become realities. But a congregation not content with being passive must make this a priority.

On the first day of a new quarter I met one of my seminary colleagues pacing the floor outside his classroom. "The first class is exciting," he said to me, "but every time I begin a new quarter I get the butterflies." Think of it, after a lifetime of teaching, he still could get nervous about his vocation! Those butterflies, I think, kept him growing and developing as a teacher! He wasn't one to "settle in." I'm not sure that teachers ever get completely comfortable with their teaching — certainly they shouldn't after an eight- or ten-hour training course. A little tension is good. It serves as an impetus for growing.

Recognizing the need for growth, teachers should be given the opportunity to attend in-service training sessions. As I talk with those responsible for Christian education, I'm often told that it's just about impossible to get teachers out for meetings. I think the key to their attendance is whether or not teachers are directly and immediately helped in their teaching. In a recent newsletter I read that teachers had requested time to meet together with others who taught the same grades. They wanted help from each other to improve their own teaching. Teachers want to do a good job. If meetings help them to teach, they will come. The pursuit of excellence should characterize teachers' meetings, and where this isn't the case, they should be canceled. Teachers don't need to be worn out attending events that aren't helpful. I think most teachers would agree to that.

Teachers in pursuit of excellence

While congregations have a responsibility to assist teachers, the pursuit of excellence is also a matter of the freedom and responsibility of the individual teacher. Not every teacher has the same strengths and weaknesses, requires the same information, or is working with the same age level. To get at their own needs, teachers will have to feel free to raise their own questions and accept responsibility for searching for answers. Simply asking the questions often serves as the prelude to the pursuit of excellence. Some questions I've heard are:

- Where do I get the stuff for . . . ?
- Has anyone around here ever . . . and how did it go?
- I'm not sure I understand what our church teaches on this subject. Can you help me?
- One of my students is terribly disruptive in class. What do you suggest I do?
- I'm not sure I dare try this activity recommended in the teachers' guide. What do you think?

What are the questions you want and need to ask? Who are the persons that you can ask? There are resource persons in every congregation who can be of assistance. Experienced church and public school teachers, pastors, and the superintendent are all possibilities. If they are to help, however, they have to be asked.

Finally, all the preparations come down to the time teachers and students have together in a class session. It's usually a very short time. In most cases it doesn't exceed one hour a week. It's not much, but we can be grateful for it and make the most of it by careful preparation. Teachers' guides and student books are marvelous aids, but they aren't so marvelous that they do away with the need for planning.

A part of my preparation is to rehearse my classes before teaching them. In my rehearsal I attempt to anticipate questions and problems that could arise. I make note of materials I will need. I try to visualize how each activity will go and if it is appropriate for the students in the class. I usually concentrate on three aspects of the session: the introduction—getting the class rolling; the transitions—connecting the various parts of the session together; and, the conclusion—checking to see if we did what we started out to do. Rehearsing a session, I've found, doesn't eliminate spontaneity and surprises from happening; it simply helps to make those surprises pleasant.

Evaluation is another way to help teachers in their pursuit of excellence. It's a subject, however, that raises red flags for many people. Evaluation is often experienced negatively—as a put-down. That is not its purpose in Christian education. Evaluation has a place only where it affirms teachers and challenges them to grow. It's my guess that most teachers already reflect, at least some, on their classes. Evaluation simply organizes these reflections a bit. For example, after a class ask yourself:

- What went right today, and what didn't? Why?
- What could I have done differently?
- Why do you suppose _____ did what she did, and _____ didn't do anything but look out the window?
- What do I need to know, or be able to do, that will enable me to enjoy teaching more?

Reflection on questions such as these is evaluation. It's far more beneficial for growth than coming out of a class and exclaiming: "Oh, I give up!" or "What a great day!" Reflection is helpful to clarify what teachers expect of themselves. These expectations give direction to growth.

A part of the pursuit of excellence has to do with expectations Christian teachers have of *themselves*. Another side of it is the expectations teachers have of their *students*. John Westerhoff says that many have described the Sunday school hour as the most wasted in the week.[5] This need not be the case—not where teachers are concerned for excellence in their teaching and have sound expectations for student learning.

49

I'm not suggesting that the Sunday school should become a religious counterpart to a student's day-school experience. Objectives, methods, and contexts may be radically different between the two. Even with those differences, there can be solid expectations for learning. One of the marks of mature teachers is that they have thought about what those expectations might be, and they strive to motivate their students to grow in them.

One thing is sure, the ministry of the church isn't served when learners get the idea that Sunday school, or any other of the church's programs, is something unimportant, something a person may take or leave. I don't suppose any teacher intends to convey that notion, but there are subtle ways it can be communicated. Striving for excellence by challenging students to grow is at least one way to avoid it.

By way of summary, take a look at the following questions. They represent a kind of evaluation. Think about your responses. What do they say about your pursuit of excellence, and that of your congregation?

1. How well do you know your students? Do you ever see them outside of the Sunday school setting?
2. How varied are the activities you use in class? When was the last time you tried something new?
3. What does the space look like where you teach? Have you done anything to brighten it up?
4. Has anyone thought about different times, places, and approaches for Christian education in your congregation?
5. When was the last time the curriculum materials were reviewed in your congregation?
6. How many in-service training sessions were offered in your congregation or conference during the past year? How many did you attend? Were they helpful?
7. How many new songs have you learned and taught to your students in the past year?
8. When was the last time teachers in your congregation got together for a Bible study or had a party?
9. When was the last time you read an article or asked a question about your vocation as a teacher?

10. How much time do you spend preparing for a class session?

Faith calls for the pursuit of excellence. The shape the pursuit takes depends on the teacher and the needs and possibilities of the congregation. When it is done in the name of Jesus, in faithful response to his love, those born to teach are made even more fruitful in the calling that is theirs.

4   *Common Sense*

". . . supplement your faith with virtue, and virtue with knowledge."   2 Peter 1:5

At the conclusion of an introductory course in education one person made the following observation: "What we've talked about this quarter is just common sense." Such a statement needs two qualifiers. One is that it is far easier to recognize common sense once it has been pointed out than when it hasn't. This, too, is common sense, but let me give an example. For literally hundreds of years teachers treated their young students as miniature adults. They were expected to sit, learn, and work as their elders did. Today, common sense dictates that children be recognized as children, with all the wonders and limitations pertaining to them. Until work had been done in the area of child growth and development, this sense was not so common.

A second qualifier is the realization that in spite of our common sense, we don't always allow ourselves to be guided by it. That's more than common sense; it's a statement about our human condition. Again, allow me an illustration. Doesn't it make sense that if church school teachers are prepared for their calling, the education program of a congregation will be improved? I think it does. Yet, how many congregations ignore the need for teacher education? Repeating the obvious doesn't make it more obvious, of course. Drawing attention to it may, however, finally lead to action. That's only common sense — and that's probably all education courses are all about.

After stating that virtue, the pursuit of excellence, is a quality of the fruitful life, the author of 2 Peter went on to make a comment that is nothing more than common sense to teachers. He wrote: "To virtue add knowledge." Nothing could be more self-evident for teachers. Knowledge is their stock in trade. That's what teachers and learners are all about. Yet, for one reason or another, it isn't always clear that knowledge has a high priority in the church, or even in the church school.

This chapter will explore several ideas about knowledge and Christian education. They appear to be so basic that one would hardly need to mention them, yet they are often ignored.

Knowledge and faith

Christian teachers are called to assist others to grow in knowledge. They are also concerned for faith. Throughout history these two— faith and knowledge — have journeyed together, sometimes as friends and sometimes not. Paul makes clear in Rom. 10:14-17 that there is a relationship between them. One can't believe in someone one knows nothing about. But how much knowledge does faith need? Is there some point at which knowledge becomes dangerous to faith?

At various times the church has apparently thought so. Several centuries ago, when Copernicus and Galileo were making their discoveries, the church censured them for what they knew. In the 19th century Charles Darwin generated fears that still rumble through the church — the fear of what knowledge may do to faith. Even theologians who press too hard for knowledge are eyed with suspicion. One young man, about to leave for the seminary, was warned by some of his friends: "Don't let them ruin your faith with all that theology."

The possibility for competition between faith and knowledge is real, and there are several reasons for it. One is the temptation to make knowledge the object of faith, a temptation no less real today than in the first century. We live in a world filled with problems. One of them that relates to many others has to do with energy. A widespread conviction is that scientists will come up with a breakthrough that will relieve us of our dependency on oil and yet allow us to live as we do now. Technology, a branch of knowledge, has become an object of hope and salvation. The capacity of knowledge to explain what previously were mysteries and to solve problems makes it a beguiling altar at which to worship.

Another reason for competition between faith and knowledge is a mistaken notion about the nature of faith. Some argue that faith is a characteristic of the human race in its infancy. When so little was known, faith was necessary to explain what could not otherwise be accounted for. Now that knowledge has provided other explanations, there is no need for faith. But, wrote Edgar Carlson, faith is not a lower kind of knowledge. Faith is not what children have because they are too young to know. Faith is:

. . . assurance and it is conviction. The testimony of the senses could not add anything to the certainty of faith. When the Christian says, "I believe in God," he is making the most confident affirmation of which he is capable.[1]

When faith is regarded as a substitute for knowledge, or when knowledge is an object of worship, Christian faith and knowledge are bound to be adversaries. On the other hand, when faith is the most confident affirmation one is capable of making, and the quest for knowledge is a journey into a more profound understanding of the faith, then faith and knowledge are the best of friends. They may not always be congenial. They may even challenge one another from time to time. But, finally, knowledge helps to make fruitful the life faith brings into being.

The problems noted above were part of the outlook of the false teachers the writer of 2 Peter accused. He was troubled both by their lack of knowledge and their tendency to enshrine it. These teachers knew about Jesus, but had either failed or refused to grasp the implications of their knowledge. They believed Jesus had freed them to live any way they pleased. The writer maintained, however, that freedom was *from* the defilements of the world, not a license to hurry back into them, as taught by the false teachers. Their problem was not in what they *knew,* but in what they *did not know*. In their ignorance of the nature of freedom, the importance of responsibility, and the relationship between faith and life, they affirmed a false conviction. These people needed *more* knowledge, not less—knowledge to help them better understand the life for which Christ had set them free.

The faith of the church was still radically new for these early Christians. Being Gentiles, they lacked the moral tradition of the Jews. How were they to understand the gospel, and what did it mean for their lives? The very questions raise a common-sense response: they had to be taught. Is there a hint of common sense here for the church of today as well? Might it not be that the issue for faith and the church is not that people know *too much* to believe, but that they know *too little?*

A second error of the false teachers addressed in 2 Peter was their tendency to make knowledge a god. The writer of 2 Peter dealt with this problem in the context of his belief in the second coming of Jesus. The false teachers denied Christ's coming on the basis of their experience. They had not seen, heard, or felt his coming, and therefore he wasn't going to come. Based on their experience they went on to assert that nothing had changed "since the fathers fell asleep" (2 Peter 3:4). They took the naive position that since they didn't know of any changes, there weren't any. "All things," they argued, "have continued as they were from the beginning of creation." In their argument they enshrined what they knew.

The author of 2 Peter insisted that they were mistaken. The world does not remain the same. It is constantly changing because God is at work within it, moving it forward to the fulfillment of God's purposes. History is not a "tale told by an idiot" that goes nowhere. It is the arena in which the purposes of God are worked out. This was the "most confident affirmation" the author of 2 Peter was capable of making.

And, of course, to enshrine the knowledge of the first century was a mistake. Those who did were not sufficiently aware of what they didn't know even to question what they did know. Today, research has penetrated into the telescopic and microscopic worlds in ways first-century scholars could not have imagined. Long-held theories about matter and the universe are repeatedly challenged. It's as the apostle Paul said in 1 Corinthians 13, our knowledge is imperfect. We can pursue it, but it is a poor god to worship. Christians believe in the God who is the Creator of the heavens and the earth. We believe it is God's future into which we are being led. We cannot go backward and find God in some previous time. We can't go back. God was there for believers in the past; God will be there as generations move into the future, however new knowledge shapes and influences the future. In faith we affirm the future as God's.

If this is what we believe, it is only common sense that we come to know more about this future and prepare for it. Unless we do, the church might enshrine what it knows today, while losing faith in the living God whose kingdom continues to come. Common sense suggests that Christian education be as concerned for faith in what God is yet to do as it is for teaching what God has already done. This seemed to make sense to the writer of 2 Peter. It helped him to keep faith and knowledge friendly.

A teacher's concern is for knowledge

There are some words that just seem to go together—words such as *teach, teachers, school, students,* and *knowledge.* Schools are places where teachers teach students, and what they teach is knowledge. While this seems to make sense, it's possible to lose sight of it. There are several reasons why it could happen—especially among teachers and students in the church school.

One reason may be that attendance at church school is voluntary. Twelve-year-olds whose parents require them to attend may dispute it, but being there has much to do with a student's motivation and the cooperation of parents. Knowing this to be true, teachers work hard to make their classes pleasant. They want their students to enjoy themselves so that they will come back each week to class. That's good, but pushed to the extreme, the measure of a class could become: "Did the students have a good time?" rather than, "Did they learn anything?"

In addition, church school teachers are expected to meet a variety of students' needs. A teacher may be called to be comforter of the small child, confidant of the growing youth, advocate of the adolescent, and friend of the adult. A teacher's ability to meet social and psychological needs may well determine how much students enjoy a class.

There's nothing wrong with making a class enjoyable and meeting students' needs. Nevertheless, when done at the expense of knowledge, the church school loses its focus. When it happens with the subtle implication that children aren't expected to learn or that learning is the opposite of enjoyment, the purpose of the church school is undermined.

Outreach and the nurture of faith are the responsibility of all Christians. No one person or aspect of the church's ministry can expect to do it all. Families, councils, choirs, committees, pastors, and teachers all work together in building up the body of Christ (Eph. 4:11-12). Teachers are called to be particularly concerned for growth in knowledge. Were they and the church school to lose this focus, where in the program of the church would it be picked up?

Another challenge to the teacher's concern for knowledge is the notion that it's a teacher's responsibility to keep students entertained and the best way to do it is to avoid stressing the learning of information. I recall an interview reported by a seminary student. He told of a young man who had quit teaching and wasn't at all hesitant about saying why. The students, he said, were just not appreciative of his efforts. The first day he met his high school class he told them that they would not be using any published materials. He wanted to be friends with them and rap about their issues and problems. He wanted them to enjoy class. By the end of the month the class was in chaos. Students and teacher had come to a position of mutual disrespect. There could have been several reasons for this failure. Among them, I think, was the belief that teachers are supposed to entertain and that there isn't really anything students want to learn.

The ability to entertain is a fine gift. Not everyone has it — not even all those who think they do. I've been in classes where teachers have tried to entertain by being funny. Not all were successful. It's especially difficult, I think, with teenagers. If it's not done well, the results are just as likely to be negative as positive.

Of greater concern is the notion that learning can't be exciting. That's not to say that learning is easy, that it doesn't require work for both students and teachers. It does. In *Jude the Obscure* Thomas Hardy tells the story of a 12-year-old boy who dreamed of going to the university. At the turn of the century, the setting of the novel, the basic entry requirement was a knowledge of Latin and Greek. Desiring to prepare himself to meet this requirement, Jude had a friend send him a grammar book for each language. When he received the package, he could hardly contain his excitement as he opened it. Then, when he looked into them, he sat down on the ground and wept. He had thought the books would provide an easy process for translating from one language into another. What he found was the necessity for memorizing the language word by word, rule by rule. For Jude it was overwhelming and discouraging.

Today, devices and materials make learning easier, but it still requires effort. Much as students and teachers may wish, knowledge doesn't come through osmosis. Nevertheless, learning can still be enjoyable. One of the surest clues to this is the excitement of children when they learn to say their first words. Even the fear involved in a child's first steps can't erase the look of elation that comes with learning to walk. Learning is a way of life for the young. The problem is not whether they will learn, but what. I've spoken with few five- and six-year-olds who didn't look forward to going to school—or Sunday school.

Unfortunately, this openness to learning tends to disappear for some as they grow older. I'm not sure anyone has figured out why this is so. It must have something to do with interests, abilities, parents, past failures and successes, opportunities, and teachers. Teachers can't account for or change all the influences others have on their students, but they can do several things. They can affirm their students in who they are and what they do know, and they can challenge them to learn more. Teachers can also help their students learn how to learn. Students who have been helped to share their own questions and taught where to look for answers are most likely to continue to be interested in learning.

Of course, it makes sense that students who enjoy their classes will look forward to coming to them. This awareness ought not be allowed to cloud the central concern of teachers—that students do come to class to learn.

A teacher's knowledge has many dimensions

During the 1960s, when schools were having many problems, one college president kept repeating one of his basic assumptions: teachers know more than their students. That makes sense—or at least I hope it does. An added assumption of the very young is that the older the students a teacher works with, the more a teacher knows.

This was brought out one day when my wife was visited in her fourth-grade classroom by the six-year-old sister of one of her students. The youngster had a question, and when my wife had given her reply, she said: "That's what my teacher told me, but I wasn't sure, so I thought I would ask you. You teach fourth grade."

It's all right, I suppose, for children to think that, but it's a mistake to think that teachers of the very young need to know little. Quite the opposite is true. A few days before the beginning of the fall term, a recent high school graduate was pressed into teaching a class of four-year-olds. She was told it would not be difficult. After all, she knew far more than the children. And, of course, she did. But she didn't know nearly enough about four-year-olds and how to work with a class of seven or eight of them. The experience was a disaster. Common sense tells us that teachers not only need to know more than their students, but also they need to know certain things that will help them in their teaching.

The more informed students become, the more able they are to raise questions. While teachers can't be expected to answer all of them, it's a problem if they can't answer any. Teachers need to know the material they are teaching—and more. One way to be prepared for a class is to read through an entire teacher's guide and student book at the beginning of a course. Many questions occur to curious students when they are introduced to a subject. Often the curriculum writer has anticipated those questions and has included them in a later session. Having read the material, teachers can either respond to the question or suggest that the student will want to be present when his question comes up in a future lesson.

A teacher's knowledge of the Bible and the Christian faith need not be based only on the curriculum materials he or she uses. As growing persons, teachers have opportunities for learning through attendance at worship services, in-service training sessions, adult Bible studies, and reading. One of the purposes of adult education is assisting teachers to know more about the faith they teach.

Another dimension of a teacher's knowledge has to do with students. In the last several decades a great deal of research has been done on how humans grow, develop, and learn. It's still a new area, and not all agree with all the results coming out of it. Nevertheless, there are insights to be gained from this study that will help a teacher to be more effective. It's only common sense for teachers to know what those insights are and to use them in their teaching.

It goes beyond my purpose here to survey principles of growth and development. There are several resources, however, that I would recommend for your study. The first is the teacher's guide. Each one has a section on what the teacher can expect from the learners for whom the materials were prepared. A brief description of age-level characteristics, from early childhood to adults, is available in the *Parish Teacher Annual,* Vol. 5 (Augsburg, 1981). I've found Iris Cully's book *Christian Child Development* (Harper & Row, 1979) extremely helpful in getting to know the child through the age of 12. *Teaching Grades Seven Through Ten,* edited by John Kerr (Parish Life, 1980), is excellent for those teaching youth and adolescents. *Christian Life Patterns* by Evelyn and James Whitehead (Doubleday, 1979) is one of the most helpful books I've read on the adult learner and Christian faith.

Plenty of materials are available on this subject. Teachers and parents will find reading them interesting and helpful. The task is to find ways to get them to those who can use them. I think it's advantageous to compare the results of research with one's own observations. With that in mind, teachers and prospective teachers should be allowed occasions when they are free to sit in a class and observe the behavior of learners. What are they interested in? What kind of things do they like to do? How long is their attention span? How do they react to each other? Much can be learned by reading and discussing, but it's amazing what can be learned simply by watching those we are called to teach. Knowing the student is an important part of a teacher's knowledge.

The sources of knowledge are another concern for church-school teachers. Some are obvious; others, often ignored. One source is the Bible. Christians confess that this book contains the revelation of God. It is the one book, above all others, that serves as a resource for Christian knowledge. Related to, and often based on the Bible, are other learning materials — student books, handouts, tapes, and filmstrips. All are sources of knowledge.

Another source is the experience of both teachers and learners. No one comes to class without some prior learning. What students know can be a valuable part of a session. In discussion, when students are allowed to talk about what they have learned, they often serve as excellent teachers for their peers. Certainly there is no rule that teachers must have a corner on all the knowledge.

The class environment is yet another source of knowledge. Posters and pictures may communicate even better than spoken words some of the concepts teachers would have their students learn. In addition, how a room looks to a student may communicate a variety of messages. Color, banners, and activity centers can transform the dreariest rooms into warm and inviting places. The way students are welcomed and included is also an important learning for them. This learning will go a long way in determining whether students conclude that church school is a place where they want to be.

Teachers are themselves one of the most important sources of knowledge in a classroom — not only in terms of information, but in being a model. More will be said of this later. It's enough to note here that teachers are something of an open book to their students. It's quite impossible for teachers to remain shadows to those they teach. We not only learn from our teachers, we learn our teachers as well.

Finally, the most important source of knowledge is the Holy Spirit. Teachers can help their students learn many things from all the resources available to them, but it is the Spirit who creates faith. Jesus said:

These things I have spoken to you, while I am still with you. But the Counselor, the Holy Spirit, whom the Father will send in my name, he will teach you all things, and bring to your remembrance all that I have said to you (John 14:25-26).

It is not difficult to recognize the variety of sources out of which knowledge comes. Teachers will want to make the most of all of them. Even more, they will pray for their students — pray that the Holy Spirit will enlighten and keep them in the faith of our Lord and Savior Jesus Christ.

Another dimension of a teacher's knowledge has to do with skills in teaching and working with a class. I would like to suggest five skills I've found helpful in my teaching — skills I wish I had when I began teaching. These skills don't guarantee a great class, but they provide a structure for thinking about, preparing for, and carrying out a teaching responsibility. What actually happens in the class can't really be predicted. In that sense, no matter what a teacher does, all efforts are experimental. And, as you know, some experiments have positive results, and some don't. Teaching is always a risk.

1. *The first skill is in identifying, writing, and working with educational objectives.* These provide the purpose and direction for what teachers and students do together. They are the basis for the selection of methods and materials. Without them there is no solid basis for evaluation. I realize that church-school teachers usually use published materials in which the objectives have already been determined. I'm not altogether sure, however, that as teachers prepare they think in terms of those objectives. The first thing I do in getting ready for a class is either to look at the stated objectives or write my own. Once I've done it, my preparations are easier and more specific.

2. *A second skill is knowing how to organize a class.* This refers to the way in which students are to relate to each other and to the teacher in a class situation. Should they work alone, in competition with each other, or cooperatively? This may not seem to be of

great importance in a church-school class of six to 12 students, but it is. In *Learning Together and Alone,* Johnson and Johnson have demonstrated that there are some things that can best be learned while students work alone, others if they cooperate in their learning, and still others if they are in competition.[2] The organization of the class depends on what the teacher would have the students learn. For example, if the objective is to have students learn some basic information about a person or place, they'll probably learn best by working alone. If they are to broaden their understanding of what the information means, the teacher might plan a discussion. If the objective is to have students learn the books of the Bible, a competitive game or drill could be most helpful. More about how to organize a class can be found in Appendix B.

3. *A third skill is choosing and using educational methods.* Methods are not the whole of teaching, but they are the means by which objectives are achieved. In a way, they are most closely related to the "performance" of a teacher, and thus need to be developed if a teacher is to be effective. When I prepare for a class, I usually think of four methods. The first is to *get the class started.* Its function is to get attention and focus on what the session will be about. How well it works has a strong influence on the rest of the class, and therefore teachers need to concentrate on it.

A second method is concerned with *communicating the material* that is to be learned. It could be a Bible story, a theological doctrine, or an issue—something students need to know if they are to accomplish the objective. One of the most difficult aspects of teaching is knowing how much material to present in a single session. Too much information, as well as too little, can lead to boredom and a short circuit of learning. Getting a feel for what students can handle comes with experience.

Getting at the meaning of the material learned is a third component of a class session that calls for a method. This method may ask students to compare what they already know with what they have just been taught. It could include an effort either to affirm or to challenge them to grow. While this activity may be as sophisticated as a case study for adults, for young children it could be going for a walk or making a collage. Whatever the activity, its purpose is to help students to think about what they have learned.

A final aspect of a session is *evaluation*. Teachers need to have some way of determining what went on in the class and whether or not the objectives were accomplished. The way it's done depends on the objectives and the nature of the class. Simple observation may tell teachers all they need to know about a particular class. At other times, projects, plays, programs, and even tests could be appropriate tools for evaluation.

When all four of these are put together—the methods for getting started, the communication of material, reflection, and evaluation—the teacher has a map that leads purposefully through a session. This map is sometimes called a lesson plan. Don't leave home for the church school without it!

4. *A fourth skill for teachers is knowing how to create a positive classroom environment.* There are at least two factors that influence classroom climate: (1) the space, and (2) attitudes existing between teachers and students and among students. The first can be taken care of with a little creative effort to make the space interesting. The second is more difficult. Of all the complaints I've heard from teachers, none is more common than lack of classroom discipline. Teachers get tired of trying to get students to "behave." As much as anything else, this fatigue leads to resignations from staff.

I wish there was a simple way to deal with this matter. Unfortunately, there isn't. Books have been written on the subject, and not all agree. How teachers manage their classes depends on their outlook and who they are. Some may prefer the position of James Dobson, as described in *Dare to Discipline* (Tyndale, 1970). Others may be more attracted to Thomas Gordon's ideas in *Teacher Effectiveness Training* (Wyden, 1974). And, even when a teacher has expressed preferences for how to handle a class, not all students respond in the same way.

Teachers often talk about discipline problems. More time should be spent talking about them *constructively*. Why are there problems, and what are some ways of dealing with them? If a situation warrants it, an in-service session could be built around this topic. In the session the views of several experts could be presented. "Old-timers" should be asked how they deal with disruptive behavior. However it is done, those responsible for recruiting and training teachers need to remember that this is an important area for teachers. Without it, their time in the classroom can be miserable.

5. *Finally, teachers need to understand the function of evaluation and how to do it.* Evaluation is a necessary, but very sensitive, area of a teacher's work. Its purpose is to assist students and teacher to grow, not to put them down. That it needs to be done with care, however, should not lead to the conclusion that it can be forgotten. It is a valuable tool and skill in helping others to grow.

All of these skills are built into the materials published for the use of teachers. It's possible to use these materials without really understanding what's behind them, but the more teachers understand what goes into the material and the more skilled they are, the more effective they will be in their teaching.

Teachers should also be concerned about the integration of information, attitudes, and behavior. This was illustrated for me in an experience I shared with children in a suburb of Los Angeles. The city leaders suggested the idea of having the schools participate in a big cleanup campaign. Materials were distributed to the schools designed to help students recognize the problems of littering. The big event came on a Saturday morning when hundreds of youngsters gathered at each school to clean the part of town assigned to them. Each child was given a large garbage bag and sent out to scour the streets, alleys, and yards for litter.

When the young folks had filled their bags, they were to bring them to the city hall and enjoy lunch provided by the city. It really was a delightful day. Hundreds participated, and more bags were filled than I would have imagined. However, there were some problems with the whole effort. As I left the city center, I saw hundreds of paper cups, used to serve the beverage for lunch, floating in a pond outside the hall. Napkins and paper plates covered the grass. One couldn't help but ask the question: what did those kids really learn? They may have learned some valuable things about civic involvement and even about the problem of littering, but I learned something too. The integration of learning is more complex than I had thought. Information, attitudes, and behavior don't come together automatically. They certainly didn't for these young people on that beautiful day in California. Yet, integration is a goal for which teachers strive. It's not enough for students to know answers to questions or be required to act in ways they don't understand. Attitudes, values, behavior, and information are all a part of knowledge; the wholeness of knowledge is called *wisdom*. Teachers, therefore, should be concerned that their students know information that is essential to their faith, but they should also be concerned about the students' attitudes toward this information and how it influences their behavior as growing Christian persons.

Is knowledge the basis for doing?

Communication is one of the key ingredients in healthy relationships. Children and youth need to know what their parents expect of them. Husbands and wives are happier when they express their love and expectations to each other. Students need to know what their teachers expect of them. It's a matter of getting things out in the open where they can be talked about and acted on.

The purpose of gaining knowledge is to have it affect the way one lives. One of the most popular definitions of learning is "a change in behavior." It seems to make sense that if a person knows something, he or she should "do it."

We realize, however, that this isn't always the way things are. Even where there is the best of communications, husbands, wives, parents, and children don't always live up to expectations—to do what they know. Though teachers go over classroom rules carefully and post them on the board, students still violate them. Teachers know much about how to teach and make their classes more interesting, but sometimes the planning and preparation gets put off. Classes are not what they could be.

Our problem is not in our lack of knowledge or the failure of our teachers. Our problem is in us: we are imperfect, we are sinners. Not all the knowledge in the world can change that—except the knowledge of God that we have in Jesus Christ. That's why he is the knowledge of greatest worth. Through faith in him, we have the forgiveness of sins. In him is the righteousness of God that makes us whole (2 Peter 1:1).

This doesn't do away with the need to learn; it does free us from the demands of perfection. In the forgiveness of sins and our forgiveness of others, relationships are restored. God's love has united us together in the one family of God. Above all else, this is what Christian teachers are called to bear witness to in their teaching. In this knowledge of God all else that is learned and taught gains its meaning.

Apart from faith this makes little sense. Yet this is the revelation we have from God. As this knowledge is added to virtue, and both are rooted in faith, Christian lives are made fruitful.

5 *The Loss of Self-Control*

". . . supplement your faith with virtue, and virtue with knowledge, and knowledge with self-control."

2 Peter 1:5-6

I can remember it as though it were yesterday. Our professor had been lecturing when one of my peers interrupted him with the remark, "That doesn't make sense." A deathly silence came over the class. All of us wondered what would happen next. Our teacher said nothing. Instead, he walked over to the window, looked out at the great out-of-doors, and slowly returned to the lectern. After what seemed like a long time he said, "That you didn't understand what I said is one thing. That it doesn't make sense is quite another. What is it you don't understand?" My colleague accepted the invitation to talk about what he didn't understand, and the rest of the class relaxed.

That episode reminds me of the value of self-control in the classroom. It's understandable how an excited student could blurt out his confusion. What a difference in the outcome, however, if the teacher had responded with anger rather than with an invitation to discuss. As it turned out, a tense and disturbing moment was transformed into a good learning situation through the exercise of self-control.

The loss of self-control can be destructive. It tends to put both teachers and students on the defensive. Where it's lacking, both say and do things that the other has a hard time forgetting. The fruitful aspects of the relationship between them are often badly bruised. No wonder the writer of 2 Peter included self-control as one of the qualities leading to a fruitful life. Certainly it's a quality to be encouraged in the growth and development of teachers.

Just what is self-control? It is not the same as "playing it cool." "Cool" persons try to stay indifferent to the feelings and moods around them. Others won't know how they feel because they conceal their feelings. While they don't seem to suffer or hurt, neither do they enjoy. It's possible for teachers to function in this way, but I can't see how it could be very satisfying. It has little to do with self-control. When emotions are eliminated, there is no need to control them.

At the same time, self-control doesn't mean that teachers have to be doormats. They don't have to accept everything their students say and do. They don't have to "take it"—whether taking it refers to their materials, their rooms, the time allowed them, or anything else that could be troubling them. Self-control is not the ability to digest the undigestible and still come out smiling as though one were simply delighted. If that's the view one adopts, one could also develop some pains—pains in the stomach. They're called ulcers.

If self-control is neither of these, what is it? Self-control, wrote Michael Green, is the capacity to direct one's emotions rather than being controlled by them.[1] One doesn't have to deny anger, joy, excitement, despair, or any other emotion. Self-control is not the elimination of feelings. It's the effort to limit their destructive tendencies—toward ourselves or others. As such, self-control is an important quality for teachers. They are in a position either to encourage or to hurt others. They are also vulnerable to the feelings of others. And how teachers and students feel about each other does influence what is learned.

Self-control has a profound effect on the fruitfulness of a teacher's ministry. Without it, students can get something of the impression of being on a roller coaster. One moment the teacher may be ecstatic, and the next shouting angrily. Roller coasters can be fun, but I'm not sure they provide much of an opportunity for learning. Riders are too busy holding on to the car and their stomachs to think much about the view. It may be the same with students who have teachers with little self-control. The emotional climate is so charged and uneven that students don't know what to expect.

As desirable as it may be, self-control is not easy to come by. Elvis Cochrane observed that it's not something we are born with, nor does it come with Baptism or conversion. He calls it a hard-earned learning.[2]

For teachers, self-control comes as the result of several things. In 2 Peter it is connected to faith, virtue, and knowledge. I'll return to this connection later. First, allow me to explore some of the causes of the disturbing loss of self-control.

Attitudes affecting a teacher's self-control

Why does a teacher lose self-control in a classroom? Why does one shout at a student or burst into tears or in some other way come unglued? One set of reasons concerns attitudes. Some people never really wanted to be teachers. Somehow they allowed themselves to be talked into it. They might even be angry about it—angry at themselves, at the pastor, or even at God. But that anger may be unleashed at students.

Another attitudinal problem arises out of the feeling of not being appreciated. Parents, the kids, the pastor—nobody seems to care. If that's the teacher's attitude — watch out!

Closely related to this is a lack of cooperation within the church school. Supplies aren't available, or someone else gets them first. Rooms are messy from another activity. Church services run overtime *again,* and there's no way to complete the lesson. Some of the teachers sit around the office drinking coffee until the last minute while *I* hurry to class to get the job done right. If a person wants to find them, it isn't hard to get steamed up over one thing or another before coming to class. Arriving in class in such a state may well be the opening movement of a disturbing situation.

Along these same lines, I think Satan works especially hard on Sunday mornings to get people unraveled before going to church. A family that gets off for school and work from Monday to Friday at 7 A.M. can somehow lose all sense of direction and time on Sunday mornings. Teachers who have felt hassled at home may find it difficult to get in tune with a class when they arrive at church.

The loss of self-control may be difficult to understand and change. The surface issue may not be the real cause. When they have had a disturbing loss of self-control, teachers would do well to think back on how they felt and what was going on. It's possible that the teacher needs to change as much as a student or the situation.

One change is to make some decisions about Sunday mornings. Getting up a little earlier, making choices about clothes the evening before, agreeing not to read the Sunday paper until after church, and having simpler breakfasts can all affect the time needed to get ready for church. Getting to the church on time without a fight could do wonders for a teacher's attitude.

Another factor is being honest with oneself and others. If teaching really makes a person miserable, that should be made known to whoever is in charge of the program. It isn't helpful for either students or teachers when anger about what they are doing goes unresolved.

Lack of appreciation can be a real issue for church-school teachers. It's not that teachers need to be coddled, but volunteers do need some assurance of the importance of what they are doing. I suggest using one meeting a year of the parish education committee to come up with ways of showing teachers appreciation. Once the ways have been decided on, do them. A fall or spring banquet is appreciated, as is the gift of a book.

A pastor friend of mine used to talk about a bonfire group in his congregation. These were the folks who would come out and support a congregational activity, no matter what it was. Teachers are like that. They are among the most loyal people in the congregation. Most often they feel a great deal of affection for one another. This should be encouraged, especially in larger congregations where all may not know one another very well. Teachers' meetings or social events that allow teachers to get better acquainted will contribute to a cooperative spirit in the church school. In Christian education, where space, time, and materials are often at a premium, cooperation is a necessity.

Behaviors affecting a teacher's self-control

Assuming that a person has been equipped in some measure to teach and work with a class, two behaviors can directly lead to a teacher's loss of self-control. One is getting to a class late. Sometimes it can't be helped, but there is no excuse for making a practice of it.

There is much to be gained by being early. Teachers who arrive early gain the opportunity of giving direction to a class before it begins. They have the freedom to organize chairs, set out materials, and in other ways control the environment before students come. As students arrive, they can be greeted and given special attention. It's a time for listening and sharing—and maybe talking with parents. Done well, this pre-class time serves as a transition into the main learning of the session. I find that when I arrive late, I talk faster, forget important details, and am overly sensitive to student behavior that may have already taken a problematical turn before I entered the door. Things go better for me when I arrive in class at least 10 to 15 minutes early.

Another behavior affecting self-control is preparation. It affects teachers because it affects students. Whether they are four years old or 40, learners aren't going to sit still and composed as teachers try to pull something together in the first five or ten minutes of a class period. If teachers aren't ready to engage their students when the time comes, students will get involved elsewhere. The energy of students, especially children, is overpowering. The teacher has to be ready to direct this energy into positive channels.

Being on time and being prepared aren't guarantees of a great class. Nevertheless, they are behaviors that can have a profound effect on students. They are a direct influence on how students behave. By taking these positive actions, teachers are less likely to experience disturbing loss of self-control.

Situations affecting a teacher's loss of self-control

There are any number of situations in which teachers may, and have, experienced a loss of self-control. The only ways I know to avoid them are either not to teach or to use only individual instruction. In such an approach to learning the amount of teacher-to-class interaction is greatly reduced. I know teachers and students can get frustrated with tape recorders and learning packets, but it's in the contact between people that situations for confrontation develop. This realization, however, should not be the basis for choosing to use an individualized approach exclusively. While individualized instruction is an effective approach, learners also need to be together if they are to accomplish the objectives of Christian education.

Surprise is one situation that leads to a teacher's loss of self-control. There are situations a teacher obviously can't control—otherwise they wouldn't be surprises. When teachers get together to talk about their work, it's the surprises that are mentioned most often. Somebody did or said something that was funny, sad, profound, or different. Surprise can be delightful. Sometimes the delight is more in retrospect than in the actual happening, but in any case, it was something the teacher couldn't make happen.

If teachers can't control surprises, what can they do to maximize their potential for joy and minimize their possibilities for disturbing a class? Again, the answer is preparation. Preparation gives a teacher confidence. It assures teachers of what they and their students are going to do and why. It allows the teacher to be surprised without being totally thrown off balance. Getting off the track is no disaster. The prepared teacher knows how and where to get back on track again, or is free to make the decision to pursue the surprise of student interest. Prepared teachers who have something worthwhile for their students to learn and do are the most likely to experience the surprise of delight—the surprise of insight and understanding.

Not every surprise in a classroom fits into the category of delight. There are also moments of disruption and even trauma—especially in action-oriented classrooms. Chairs tip, jars fall and break, watercolors get spilled, clothes get torn, words are said, little children have "accidents." They happen because active people are there doing something. They happen, and teachers have to respond to them.

Teachers who overreact to these kinds of surprises are going to have students who do the same—and that spells nothing but trouble. Teachers should "expect the unexpected" and "accept the unexpected." Avoid as much as possible taking whatever happens personally — unless, of course, a failure to prepare and think it through was the cause. You can accept surprises more easily if you have a sense of humor and the capacity not to take yourself too seriously. These may be traits of the born teacher. They also develop as teachers grow in what they know and understand about themselves, their students, and their calling to teach.

Teachers may also lose self-control when they are threatened or challenged. Students can challenge teachers in terms of what they know about the subject they are teaching. It may take the form of a question: "Is that really true?" or "Didn't you say something different last week?" or "Why can't we do something that is fun once in a while?" On the other hand, the challenge may take the shape of a statement: "I don't believe that!" or "That's not what we've been taught before!" or "That's not what my dad says!" Still worse might be the combination of the two: "Oh, this is dumb! Why do we have to learn it?"

How is a teacher to respond to statements and questions like these? How do you respond? Does your response vary—depending on who the student is and how you are feeling at the time? Which of the following might be characteristic of you?

"You don't know what you're talking about. Just listen and pay attention."
"Thanks for raising the question. What do some of the others of you think?"
"What we're talking about isn't dumb. What makes you think it is?"
"That's an interesting question. Where might we look for an answer?"
"I'm correct in what I've been saying. Let's both check it out, though, before class next week."
"You should listen to what God has to say. Don't you care what God thinks about you?"
"One more stupid remark like that and you're going to have to leave this class. Do you understand me?"

The responses teachers give to the challenges of students are closely related to the attitudes teachers bring with them to class and their understanding of themselves, their students, and their calling.

Teachers also are challenged in terms of who is in charge of the class. Some students seem to have a need for checking this out. They want to know how much they can get away with, what the boundaries are, and who's in charge. If a teacher isn't prepared to lead, one or another of the students may be—and that may cause disturbances in a class. It's a basic cause for behavior problems that lead to a teacher's loss of self-control. The best antidote to behavior problems is not allowing them to develop—and while that is easier said than done, it is directly related to a teacher's understanding of self, students, and teaching.

Parents can also pose a challenge or threat to church-school teachers. Teachers usually want parents to be involved in their child's learning. When parents get interested, they may become critical. Some may be negative if they think there isn't enough concentration on the Bible. Others may think just the opposite. Materials, the hour for Sunday school, the personality of the teacher, the location of the room, the size of the class—all these may provoke a parental challenge. Pastors hear many of the same criticisms with respect to confirmation instruction. How teachers respond to parental challenges may reflect what's been going on in their lives that day. It'll also depend on who they are, what they know about their students, and their skills as a teacher.

The more able teachers are in using the skills of their craft, the fewer are the demands placed on their self-control. By being well-informed on the subject, broadly equipped with the skills described in the previous chapter, and prepared for the particular session, teachers are ready for surprises and challenges and probably won't be overwhelmed by them.

In the teacher's guide for three-year-olds that I have before me, the writer tells the teacher to prepare at least two, and preferably three, interest centers. They are to be ready for use when the children enter the class. The writer has suggested five simple activities from which the teacher may choose. What will happen when the teacher reads this? One possibility is that it will be ignored. The teacher might say, "That's too much work," or "I don't know where to find all that stuff," or "Why do those kids need all three activities?" With this sort of rationalizing, activities for the class are not prepared.

On the other hand, teachers who know something of three-year-olds and the activities appropriate for them will start to look around for the objects they will need and wonder about how they will be able to set them up in the space available in their rooms. Other teachers may like the idea but have some activities of their own they would like to use.

When class time comes, you can guess which classes are most likely to go well, and the one that isn't. In the first, those busy little boys and girls are going to be moving around, doing all sorts of things—most of them unplanned. The more directions in which they go, the more tense the teacher could become—and before long there's the possibility of the loss of self-control. Genuine surprises aren't predictable, but I think this one is no surprise. Congregations that don't provide for teacher training before placing persons into a classroom are contributing to situations that lead to the loss of self-control. Teachers who don't allow themselves opportunities to grow in their skills and knowledge are ignoring one of the keys that could keep them from this disturbing loss.

Teachers and students are both saints and sinners. This understanding is significant for a teacher's self-control. What it means is that teachers know where their worth comes from — the grace of God in Jesus Christ. They don't have to be perfect, or know all the answers, or even be always composed in a class. Challenges, questions, and disruptive behavior need not rob them of their worth. They are the beloved and forgiven ones. In their acceptance of God's love, they are able to love and accept themselves. In God's victory they don't have to win every encounter in class. Set free in Christ, they don't have to be defensive about themselves, what they do or don't know, or how bright they might be. Challenges to authority will not be seen as a personal threat to one's ego.

Teachers are God's people who by God's grace have been called to a ministry. It is a ministry with problems and difficulties. Faith in God and God's love, confidence in God's calling to ministry, and enthusiasm for the mission of the church are the resources from which teachers draw when their self-control is being challenged. Prayer—before, during, and after teaching—brings these resources into reality as teachers go about their work. And, when control is lost, grace is the way to forgiveness for oneself and the source of strength for restoring relationships between teachers, students, and parents.

At the same time, being saints, teachers have rich opportunities for being witnesses to the grace and power of God as they live out their faith—teaching and forgiving, just as they have been taught and forgiven.

Students, too, are saints and sinners. Teachers can expect challenges, not because teachers aren't able, but because students aren't perfect. They come to class with a variety of needs and moods. Sometimes they are going to be disruptive. Teachers don't deal with this in the best way when they engage in open combat—shouting, sarcasm, or other forms of a loss of self-control. When they do, teachers only add to an already disturbing situation, which can have negative consequences for any fruitful relationships in the class. A teacher who practices self-control may be "good news" for a student who has become accustomed to being put down. And, when anger has had its way, the giving and asking for forgiveness may communicate more effectively than anything else what Christian education is all about.

If students can challenge a teacher's self-control, they can also be a great source of delight. Given opportunity, they are filled with surprises that reflect the glory and grace of God within them—whatever their ages might be.

The author of 2 Peter connected faith, virtue, knowledge, and self-control. Self-control begins in faith—faith in the love of God, which daily renews the lives of God's people. It continues as teachers pursue excellence in their calling. Knowledge of self, of students, and of teaching skills make their contribution to self-control. In its turn, self-control allows virtue and knowledge to be fruitful in the relationship between teachers and their students.

6 *Stability and Steadfastness*

". . . supplement your faith with virtue, and virtue with knowledge, and knowledge with self-control, and self-control with steadfastness." *2 Peter 1:5-6*

Contemporary education and fashions have something in common. Both can be very much affected by fads. Fads are characterized by short duration and exaggeration. They are pursued for only a short time and with exaggerated zeal.

We live in an age of education innovations. Some of the words and phrases describing these innovations are *individualized instruction, back-to-the-basics, values clarification, intergenerational learning, cooperative learning centers, modular scheduling, age-graded materials,* and *computer-assisted education.* Some may qualify as fads simply because they have been adopted with great enthusiasm and then, after a short time, discarded for another innovation.

One example of this is the open classroom. In some communities the decision was made to tear down the walls between classes in order to create the space for openness. After a few years what began with great exhilaration ended in some places with disappointment. Masons were called back, and the walls were rebuilt. The open classroom may not have received a fair trial. The design was often put into use without really equipping teachers in how to work with and in it. Perhaps that's a characteristic of educational fads: they are theories and practices that are tried and discarded before they are given a chance to prove themselves.

Fads in education can contribute to unevenness and confusion in programs. This unevenness can result in disruptions and low morale for both teachers and learners. It inhibits growth.

Because of more limited financial resources, Christian education may not have the opportunity of being as innovative as public education. But congregational programs for education have their own problems with unevenness. Some of these problems may be the result of deliberate decisions to follow fads. Others may be caused by lack of leadership and stability in the church school.

There can be no doubt that variety is a great aid to learning. It is a source of motivation and interest for both teachers and learners and a sign of their growing. But too much variety, too many changes, may be a liability. While learning thrives on new experiences and challenges, it also needs a measure of stability. Peter refers to this quality as *steadfastness*. It's a quality that he commends for the fruitful life.

The writer of 2 Peter would not—nor would I—want to be seen as a defender of those last seven words of the church: "We never did it that way before." Nevertheless, his inclusion of steadfastness in the list of qualities leading to a fruitful life indicates his concern for stability as a contributing factor in growth. For the church school, stability is important in curriculum materials, organization, and staff.

Steadfastness in the use of materials

An editor of educational resources made the following observation: "When something goes wrong in public education, it's usually

84

the teacher who is held responsible. When there are problems in the church school, the problem is with the materials."

Educational resources are important. Teachers need to have confidence in them. Choosing which ones to use is one of the most critical decisions made in the church school. That decision should be made after an evaluation process involving parents, teachers, parish education committee members, students, and pastors. The process should include a fair look at alternatives—from both denominational and nondenominational publishers. Once a decision is made, for the sake of stability it should be upheld for a given period of time. In one congregation I served we agreed, after an evaluation, that we would not review the materials in a formal way for three years. At the congregation's annual meeting we asked for and received support for this decision. That gave us three years of stability —and time to look at other issues in the church school.

Several reasons can be given for maintaining some stability in this area. One is continuity. In planning curriculum materials, editors are guided by long-range goals. Biblical stories are repeated from time to time with the awareness that students will grasp new insights in the stories as they mature in their ability to conceptualize. Theological themes are introduced and reinforced over a period of several years. Commitment to these themes throughout the curriculum reduces the possibilities for theological confusion and contradictions. Stability in the use of materials allows learners to grow toward some of these long-term goals.

Stability in materials is also helpful to teachers. In my teaching I'm often given an opportunity to repeat a class and to make changes in the second that occurred to me while I was teaching the first. Repeating a class allows the teacher to get beyond the survival stage and into evaluation and enrichment. Teachers who use the same material for several years would do well to keep a journal on their teaching. The journal could be a great asset when the time comes to repeat a session. It can remind the teacher of those things that went well, the problem areas, and the ideas that were generated during the teaching. Although materials are used again, the class need not be the same year after year. When the main outline for the session is already decided, teachers can concentrate on fine-tuning it.

Another reason for stability is that it allows for recycling materials. As in all recycling efforts, this involves a collection point and a system for retrieval. It takes some time in establishing both, but it's worth it. I know of one person whose "only" job is to collect, file, and retrieve materials for teachers—pictures, filmstrips, objects, etc. In addition, many teachers keep files or boxes in which to gather their recyclables. Knowing the topics for the coming year, because they are the same ones as for the present year, makes the collecting all the easier. (Along with collecting there needs to be some way of weeding out the stuff that isn't used. Too much material is about as bad as too little.)

Related to recycling is cost efficiency. Repeated use of a teacher's guide, filmstrips, and other materials help to keep costs down—especially if the materials are kept in a place where they can be found from one year to the next. Money saved can then be used in other ways to enrich the program of education in a congregation.

Steadfastness in terms of organization

Organization is a broad term that refers to many aspects of a congregation's educational program. It includes the times and places for educational opportunities as well as the approaches that are used. All are important considerations. Decisions made with respect to them often reflect a congregation's priorities.

Three approaches that have received considerable attention of late are individualized instruction, intergenerational learning, and caring communities. My experience with each of these approaches has been both positive and negative. They provide an excellent opportunity for different kinds of learning and for variety in an educational program. At this point, none of them seems to be the panacea. Any of them can be carefully incorporated into the overall program of a congregation. Those who want to implement them, however, should be aware that they require more effort rather than less. For that reason, more time in planning, more thought to possibilities and problems, and more conversations with the people involved are necessary than with a traditional approach. My experience is that where this isn't the case, the variation turns out to be an intrusion rather than an enrichment to learning.

Especially in a busy congregation, scheduling can be difficult. An innovative, creative group of people is always coming up with new ideas and possibilities for ministry. Some of these are bound to conflict with times for Christian education. Choirs, Scout groups, committee meetings, additional worship services, community-service groups—all compete for times and space with the educational program. Sunday mornings present the challenges of more committee meetings, coffee hours, and special programs. All of these can be good.

All of these, however, need to be seen in perspective. Because of varying interests, some people within a congregation may have difficulty in recognizing the difference between their concerns and the mission of the church. The granting of space and time often reflects a congregation's priorities and is therefore an area for confrontation. Strong leadership on the part of pastors and church councils is needed to keep the mission of the church in focus and to minimize negative consequences when conflicts develop.

Unfortunately, education is sometimes taken for granted. It's one of those things that's always there and always will be. Therefore, it's all right to juggle its time or place, or even to call it off if something more exciting comes along. That can be very frustrating. It interrupts the rhythm of teachers in their preparations. It communicates to students that learning is not very important.

Stability and predictability should characterize a congregation's educational efforts. If the church is understood as the community in which the gospel is preached and taught and the sacraments administered, this stability should not be hard to defend.

Steadfastness in scheduling must first take into account people. Education and scheduling are for people, not the other way around. When making organizational decisions, both the needs of people and the needs of the church must be taken into account. Steadfastness, seen as this kind of commitment, may well require a congregation to be flexible in some ways. Even here, however, I recommend the following when making decisions about changes in organizational structure and scheduling:

1. Make changes thoughtfully. Are they a response to a squeaky wheel or to the legitimate needs of people?
2. Involve others in the decision—especially those who will be influenced by any changes.
3. Consider how changes will affect other programs and people in the congregation.
4. How does the decision reflect the stated priorities of the congregation?
5. Explore the possibilities of doing innovative activities within existing structures.
6. Publicize changes made in as many ways as possible.
7. Be prepared to accept the fact that someone won't like the change. Therefore, be responsible for your decision.

Steadfastness in terms of staff

In his commentary on 2 Peter, Elvin Cochrane suggests that steadfastness carries the meaning of courage—a voluntary and daily enduring of difficult and hard things for the sake of usefulness.[1] That may not be quite the picture one would want to convey of teaching in the church, but it does have to be a part of it. Teaching implies a person who is growing—and growth is a continuing process that includes struggle and difficulties. Teachers will have many good reasons for celebrating, but there are also times that call one to endure, to remain steadfast in one's calling for "the sake of usefulness."

Steadfastness is a condition for a teacher's growth. As they face their first class, teachers often wonder what in the world they are doing there. If the class goes well, the teacher will probably look forward to next week. If it doesn't, some may look for a place to drop their materials—and quit. Whether teachers continue to grow depends on whether they come back to the class and stay with the task over a period of time. Being steadfast in this situation isn't only a matter of one's own self-resolve. Much depends on the training that went on before the first class and the kind of support that teachers sense as they grow.

Steadfastness contributes to the development of community and belonging. Teachers who have been together over several years may develop a spirit of camaraderie. They are together in mission. They share the same concerns, interests, students, and stories. While one would not want to create a closed atmosphere, this is a ministry in which people can experience a rich measure of belonging—if they remain steadfast. Even in this time of mobility, church-school teachers who transfer to another congregation and take up their calling there find a bond that exists among all teachers who are steadfast.

Belonging is also important for students. Because Christian education is relational, steadfastness is an important part of it. A constant turnover of teachers and staff makes it difficult for trust to develop—trust which is so important to sound relationships. Some might even want to explore the possibilities of promoting teachers with their students for several years in order that relationships be continued. This eliminates the positive values of repetition with materials, but it allows for continuity with people.

Steadfastness calls for commitment—a commitment to both people and teaching. Commitment can be understood in a variety of ways. One that seems to threaten many prospective teachers is the notion of having "to be there" every session, especially when the class meets on Sunday. Like it or not, in our mobile society, neither students nor teachers are eager to commit themselves to every Sunday over a long period of time. People being together in a class on a regular basis is very important, but commitment includes more than places, times, and scheduled programs. It includes people and learning. Seen this way, commitment can be shared by all those in a congregation responsible for Christian education—not just the teacher.

For example, where there is a commitment to learning, alternatives to Sunday school can be provided for those students who are away from their home church on a particular weekend. Packets could be prepared for students to check out for use when they are away. Included in the packets could be both family and individual learning activities. There could be stories to be read, or listened to on tape, as the family travels. There could be songs for listening to and singing, puzzles, car games, and other activities for a family on the move. If a congregation is committed to learning, it won't matter where or when it happens. Besides, developing some packets as I've suggested could be fun. It would be a chance to use some of those educational innovations mentioned earlier — family, intergenerational, and individualized learning.

Commitment to learning may also require more work in developing a teaching staff. I've heard suggestions that teachers be allowed to commit themselves for only a month or two out of a year, and then be free of their responsibilities. I'm not so sure that I prefer that approach. I can understand, however, a teacher's wanting to be free to be away from class one Sunday a month. Making this possible extends commitment beyond the few individuals who are able to be there every Sunday to the larger body of the congregation and its educational leadership. Why should steadfastness be expected only of the organist, the choir, pastors, and a few Sunday school teachers? Being steadfast implies an ongoing effort in selecting and training teachers. It means creating a positive and vibrant attitude toward learning throughout the congregation. It means searching for alternative ways of handling teaching responsibilities in the church school: team teaching, shared teaching, clustering, teacher aids, parallel teaching, to name a few. Any approach has to allow for the development of a sense of belonging—of community. Community requires the commitment of people to be together over an extended period of time, but it doesn't require perfect attendance.

Steadfastness in learning needs to run through faith communities as well as individuals called teachers. It implies an ongoing high priority on teaching and learning, a continuing emphasis on the selection and training of teachers, and a willingness to look for and implement structures that allow both teachers and students to be steadfast in their calling.

Steadfastness is not a quality that stands by itself. It is interrelated with others—all of which, together, contribute to the fruitful life. Self-control and steadfastness are closely linked. It would be hard to imagine the development of one without the other. Part of the capacity to endure rests in knowing why it is being done. Knowledge, whether it is of the "greatest worth" or any of the skills required of a teacher, assists one to be steadfast in teaching. The continuing pursuit of excellence is impossible without endurance. And, like all the qualities with which it is linked, a teacher's steadfastness is rooted in the faithfulness of God. God is the one who is "the same yesterday, today, and forever" (Heb. 13:8). God is the one whose promises are ever sure, unshakable, eternal. It is God's love that endures from age to age.

Martin Lange and Reinhold Iblacker reported an interview with Paraguayan *campesinos,* who were asked where their strength came from to continue the struggle of developing a community where they could have food to eat, shelters in which to live, and freedom to worship God. The interviewers found that "Their strength was in their deep faith, truly incorporated into their lives." [2] These courageous farmers reflect Elvis Cochrane's comments about the relationship between faith and steadfastness. "It is," he wrote, "in reliance upon God, obedience to his will, trust in his goodness, the results of knowledge in faith, that we are enabled to persevere with steadfastness." [3]

Out of the rich resources of God's grace, received in faith, teachers are enabled to be steadfast in their calling. Likewise, congregations are enabled to persevere in searching for ways that go beyond fads and convenience to express their commitment to teaching and learning, teachers and learners. In this shared commitment the fruitfulness of individuals and communities of faith is enhanced.

7 An Example of Godliness

*". . . supplement your faith with virtue, and virtue
with knowledge, and knowledge with self-control, and
self-control with steadfastness, and steadfastness with
godliness."   2 Peter 1:5-6*

"Give me an example" is a phrase every teacher has heard. It's usually a plea for some specific illustration that will help students to understand what they are being taught. Sometimes the example is a story or personal experience. At other times a teacher may use a word or phrase students already know to clarify a new idea they are trying to communicate. The second letter of Peter attempts to illustrate what is meant by a fruitful life. In this attempt, the writer did not tell many stories, though he did allude to some good ones (like one about Balaam's ass). And, he didn't refer to any personal experiences other than that on the Mount of Trans-figuration. He used words to illustrate his conception of the fruitful life, assuming that his readers would know what he meant by them.

The fruitful life, as the author of 2 Peter described it, looked like a life lived in *pursuit of excellence,* a life informed by *knowl-*

edge, a life of *self-control,* and a life that is *steady.* Each of these words, in turn, implied behaviors. To a large extent, the writer left it to his readers to tell their own stories and experiences that would make these behaviors explicit.

There is always a risk in responding to the request, "Give me an example." The risk is that the example becomes the norm in understanding the concept being explained. The description of the fruitful life in 2 Peter could be misunderstood as *the* expectation of all faithful people. Nothing in 2 Peter's characterization contradicts faith, but if it were to become the norm, so much having to do with faith would be excluded. The problem would be similar to the one Jesus saw in the Pharisees—a life with boundaries. Living with boundaries can be a source of security. It can also serve as a justification for staying within them even when the love of God calls one out. That's legalism.

Though this risk is present, one can't avoid the use of examples— not unless one is content to say that there is no way to illustrate how faith and life are related. Whatever risks are involved in giving examples of virtue or self-control, they are increased when it comes to the term *godliness.* For that reason it's a controversial word. Not that anyone is against it, or that godliness doesn't belong in a description of the fruitful life, but *godliness,* or *piety,* as the word in 2 Peter is sometimes translated, carries with it many preconceived notions and biases. Some people get nervous just talking about it, afraid that examples given to illustrate it might become normative for all. Misunderstandings about godliness have led to self-righteousness and judgmentalism. That being the case, there is all the more reason for those called to teach to think about this good word.

The author of 2 Peter is better at describing what godliness isn't than what it is. That's not surprising, because this letter is an argument against the teaching and practice of false teachers. After describing them the writer asked his readers: "What sort of persons ought you to be in holiness and godliness" (2 Peter 3:11). At first glance he appears to have given no answer to his question. He assumes that his readers know what holiness and godliness mean. However, as one examines the letter more carefully, it becomes evident that godliness is one of its central themes—the godly life that is an expression of faith in the Lord and Savior Jesus Christ.

Faith and life

Perhaps the false teachers we meet in Peter would not have been asked, or allowed, to teach in any church school. Teachers aren't perfect, but the kind of gross immorality described in 2 Peter seems extreme, even in this modern age. Nevertheless, 2 Peter does point to a concern for those called to teach: the relationship between faith and life. What is taught about that connection is, itself, a matter of godliness for teachers. A wrong understanding of it led to ungodliness.

The author of 2 Peter was convinced that Jesus had both saved the world from sin and called it to a life transformed by the gospel. It was the connection between the two that the false teachers denied. They spoke of freedom in the gospel and very likely of the forgiveness of sins. At the same time, they used the gospel as a justification for allowing them to live as they pleased—to have all the "fun" without paying any of the cost. Jesus, they seem to have argued, had paid the price that made it possible for them to do as they pleased, even if that meant adultery and the exploitation of others. Not only was this the doctrine that guided their own behavior, it was in the content they taught.

For, uttering loud boasts of folly, they entice with licentious passions of the flesh men who have barely escaped from those who live in error. They promise them freedom, but they themselves are slaves of corruption; for whatever overcomes a man, to that he is enslaved. For if, after they have escaped the defilements of the world through the knowledge of our Lord and Savior Jesus Christ, they are again entangled in them and overpowered, the last state has become worse for them than the first (2 Peter 2:18-20).

95

By denying the relationship between faith and life, the false teachers concealed the witness to the transforming power of God both in themselves and those they taught. God's purpose in the gospel is to set people free. The effect of the false teachers was just the opposite—slavery. God's purpose is to recreate and give new life to the world he has made. Destruction followed the false teachers (2:1). God's purpose is to reveal his love and to give the gift of salvation. To be witnesses to that in faith and life is to be godly.

Implications for teaching and learning

Those called to teach are representatives of the gospel. The good news is that God, apart from any merit in humankind, redeemed the world. The mission of the church is to make this message known and to call people to faith. The announcement of the gospel, however, does not allow for a separation of faith and life. God's gift of salvation is intended for wholeness—not a life divided against itself. Jesus, Paul, James, and Peter all spoke out against those who argued for such a division. From both a religious and logical point of view, attempts to separate faith and life seem as perverse as they are persistent. One can't help but empathize with Paul when he wrote: "What shall we say then? Are we to continue in sin that grace might abound? By no means! How can we who died to sin still live in it?" (Rom. 6:1-2). In the following an attempt is made to illustrate, from an educational perspective, how these two—faith and life—are related.

Faith and action

Faith seeks understanding, and understanding seeks faith. These are two significant and well-traveled approaches to discovering what it means to believe. The concern of godliness might be phrased somewhat differently: Faith seeks action, and action seeks faith. Let me explain by giving an example of each of these from the life of the apostle Paul.

Paul was not hesitant to write or speak of his life experiences. In Acts we read of the many times Jews in the synagogues would not listen to his preaching. This contributed to his growing conviction that he was sent to preach to the Gentiles. Although there must have been times of beautiful refreshment in the life of Paul, he had his share of frustration. But out of those experiences he learned to be content in whatever state he found himself (Phil. 4:11). It is an expression of faith confirmed in life.

On the other side, Paul fervently believed that he had been called to be a servant of the gospel. That faith supported him in every situation. There must have been times in his life when he wanted to call it quits as a preacher and teacher, but he couldn't. The love of God constrained him to be about his calling (2 Cor. 5:14). In response, Paul's faith—or at least the scope of his mission with respect to it—grew.

Teachers need to make a deliberate effort to include action as part of the content in Christian education. Action needs to be informed by the reflections of faith, and faith seeks to express itself in action.

Learning by doing

John Dewey didn't formulate the idea, but he popularized the phrase "learning by doing." He maintained, as many before him, that we learn what we do. It wasn't quite that simple, according to Dewey. To learn, beyond habitual behavior, one also had to reflect on (think about) one's behavior. And Dewey didn't mean that doing always required one to be moving around with one's body. The mind is capable of doing too.

Even with those qualifications, the effect of physical doing on learning is considerable. A study done to measure what students remembered found that what is seen, heard, said, and done is best remembered.[1] If that's true, then a place for doing must be found in Christian education.

If remembering the Exodus is important, ways must be found for doing it—perhaps through dramatization. But some dimensions of the Christian faith are not as easy to act out as the Exodus. These are the abstractions like love, trust, compassion, joy, forgiveness, and mercy. Jesus clarified words like these by telling stories. We often do the same. It should be pointed out, however, that after telling the story of the good Samaritan as an example of love for one's neighbor, Jesus said: "Go and do likewise" (Luke 10:37). Jesus wanted more for his listeners than a clearer understanding of love. Love is a sign of the coming kingdom, the kingdom Jesus brings. Jesus used words to encourage the expression of love, but may have been suggesting that in *doing* the acts of love, people would discover its meaning in a more profound way than if they only heard about it.

One can talk about compassion in terms of people who have needs, but it takes action to make the word real. This is true for the one receiving it as well as the one doing the act of compassion. The same can be said for many other Christian qualities. Until one has forgiven or shown mercy one doesn't really know what these words represent.

If God is actively compassionate, loving, forgiving, and merciful, then to know God is to know something about what these words signify—to know them through one's actions. It could be argued, as Amos did, that those who do acts of justice are closer to knowing God than those who only talk about him (Amos 5:21-24).

What does all this have to say about teaching? Among other things, it means providing opportunities for behavior that assists learning and retention. One example is the confirmation program of an inner-city congregation in New York City. After they are confirmed, the students are expected to participate in the life and mission of the congregation. They go with the pastor on hospital and home visitations. They join with the pastor in prayer for people and their needs. Beyond helping these young people to identify with the mission of the church, this pastor hopes that they will gain a deeper understanding of the love of God.

There's hardly a teacher's guide written these days that doesn't plan for some student activity. For the very young the activity may point to a concept far beyond the comprehension level of the learner. Yet, through carefully chosen activities, students can learn and express something of their relationship with God. Sofia Cavalletti's book *The Religious Potential of the Child* demonstrates this. [2]

Sometimes the activities found in the teacher's guide are perceived as filler, something to be done after all the important teaching and learning has been taken care of. And some activities may be ignored because they are complicated by the need for space or materials. For a variety of reasons, doing may not seem to be very important for learning. But one of the ways we and our students learn is by doing. This is true also of godliness. That being the case, activities designed to assist learning have to be given a place in the church school and done with care.

Teaching by doing

In the past there was no similar problem with respect to teaching by doing. It was assumed that a great deal was learned by imitation —by students following the example of their teachers. Guided by that principle, teachers were carefully screened in terms of their behavior. If their doing was inconsistent with their saying, they were disqualified from office.

Whether out of modesty or an unwillingness to serve as models, some teachers have argued that they should not be accountable for what their behavior may teach. That's especially true of their behavior outside the classroom. They don't want to be held up as examples of right living. Richard John Neuhaus asserts that this viewpoint is held by some pastors and teachers of the church, who maintain that they are like everyone else and therefore more ought not to be expected of them than others. That argument is invalid, Neuhaus contends: "Is the burden of being different unfair? Not really; not if we have freely affirmed the vocation and pledge to adorn the gospel with a holy life." [3]

The writer of 2 Peter would have agreed with Neuhaus. He was convinced that the behavior of false teachers did influence what believers and unbelievers knew about the church and Christian faith. Observing this behavior, the world was scandalized by it. Thus, rather than attracting people through the love of Christ, these false teachers were driving them away by their licentious behavior. No word more aptly describes them than *ungodly*. At the same time, their behavior confused believers. They were enticed into emulating their teachers and thereby lost the stability of their faith. Peter was convinced that consistent ungodly behavior led to the erosion of faith—either one's own or that of another.

Several examples can be cited to support the idea of teaching by doing. The incarnation of our Lord Jesus speaks volumes about it. Paul pointed to the cross and exhorted: if you want to know how much God loves you, see what he has done for you; while you were yet sinners, he died for you (Rom. 5:8).

Jesus told stories to illustrate much of what he taught. But when he wanted to illustrate to both children and adults that he welcomed all, he acted. He took children into his arms and blessed them. Children may not know much of the meaning of abstractions, but actions associated with them do communicate a message. A touch, a hug, a smile, a welcoming gesture, a soft word, the satisfying of a need, a comforting presence—all provide substance for the definition of love in the mind of a child. Iris Cully states that the first learnings in Christian education come early in life. They are related to the complicated and significant learnings of trust—and they come through the actions of parents or their representatives.[4]

In a graduate school classroom the teacher had been trying to get a discussion started on an assigned reading. As one member of the class after another admitted to not reading the material, the instructor became increasingly disturbed. Finally, after one student facetiously remarked: "Hey, you wouldn't want me to be any different, would you?" the teacher lost his temper. "No," he replied sarcastically, "nor would I want you to go beyond the bounds of stupidity and arrogance, but you have." Whatever humor might have been present in the class quickly disappeared. Somehow the class ended. As class members left, the teacher asked the one to whom he had spoken sharply to remain for a moment. He apologized for his words spoken in anger and asked to be forgiven. On an evaluation form filled in by students at the end of the term there was this comment: "It was good to be in a class where a teacher can apologize and ask for forgiveness. It was a good learning."

What is it that students learn from our doing as teachers? Obviously they don't learn the way of perfection. At the same time, I hope we aren't studies in gross immorality. The words of Neuhaus are a good guide—that from their teachers students learn something of a holy life that adorns the gospel. That's a godly life and a blessing to those who learn from it.

Godliness and teachers

Godliness refers to the way we live as an expression of the faith God has given. Living the faith is the calling of every Christian. To be godly is to reflect in one's life what we know of the qualities of God: love, compassion, goodness, mercy, holiness, creativity, generosity, and justice. Because of factors involved in teaching and learning, godliness is of special concern for those called to teach.

Are there any behaviors that are especially appropriate for teachers? There are some that can serve as a basis for discussion, as long as they do not become the boundaries of what teachers do. The first list of qualities comes from a teacher who died in the midst of doing her ministry in El Salvador. When Sister Carol was asked to name the most important qualities of a teacher, she responded:

- an attitude of continuous learning
- an attitude of listening
- an attitude of half-failure
- an attitude of questioning
- an attitude of prayer
- an attitude of being a sinner sent to sinners
- an attitude of being poor [5]

How could these attitudes influence the behavior of teachers, and in what ways do they illustrate godliness?

When educational leaders in the United Methodist Church wanted some information about teacher expectations, they asked learners. They found the following to be most consistently noted:

- showing up for class
- being dependable
- being trustworthy in doing routine things
- willing to listen to learners
- willing to repeat basic truths
- willing to work with learners [6]

These expectations are simple; yet they have the potential of becoming examples of godliness in the faith and life of teachers.

8 *The More Excellent Way*

". . . supplement your faith with virtue, and virtue with knowledge, and knowledge with self-control, and self-control with steadfastness, and steadfastness with godliness, and godliness with brotherly affection, *and brotherly affection with* love."   *2 Peter 1:5-7*

When teachers were asked to list those qualities they thought to be the most essential for teaching in the church, *faith* and *love* were the only two that were included by all. That's not surprising, since these are central themes in both the Old and New Testaments. Few, if any, words were more on the lips of Jesus. And when Paul commended a more excellent way to the believers in Corinth, he described for them the way of love.

In 2 Peter, the qualities that make for the fruitful life begin with *faith* and end with *love*. Virtue, knowledge, self-control, steadfastness, and godliness find their foundation in faith and their motivation in love.

Biblical scholars, most notably Anders Nygren, have distinguished between the two words that the author of 2 Peter used to close his list: *phileo* (brotherly love) and *agape* (love). Without denying that these distinctions exist, the two terms are dealt with together here. Both are taken to mean, as G. Johnston has suggested, a "genuine good will that puts first the needs and interests of the other." [1]

At first glance the epistle of 2 Peter doesn't seem to have much to say about love defined in this way. As a matter of fact, it is an angry letter. The concern here was for false teachers and the effect they were having on the early church. In words that could never be called gentle their motives and actions were exposed as destructive of themselves and those who followed them. The writer saw nothing of goodwill in them. Their intent was to put themselves before all others—even God. Yet, 2 Peter does have some things to say about love for the one called to teach.

To love is to receive and give

One of the most severe criticisms that the writer of 2 Peter brought against the false teachers was their closed-mindedness, their unwillingness to be instructed. He found that when their opinions and experiences were in opposition to the apostolic tradition, the false teachers rejected the tradition. When the challenges of living a life worthy of their calling conflicted with how they wanted to live, they followed their own way. These false teachers claimed the right to pick and choose what they wanted to hear and respond to, discarding what didn't appeal to them.

With that outlook it is doubtful that they ever heard the gospel. The writer especially pointed out their rejection of the hope that Christ will come again in power. He understood that denial as a rejection of the purpose and promise of God and the basis for their claim that they were free to live as they wanted. With no future dimension to their lives, they lived in the present as ones who had no allegiance except to their own desires and opinions.

Closed to the gospel, these false teachers had little or nothing to give their students. They were "waterless springs and mists driven by a storm" (2 Peter 2:17). What they taught had no substance

104

or lasting value. They created and offered to others mirages that disappeared when confronted by life's realities. This is the cruelest of deceptions—to lead others to think they have been given something of great value, only to discover that they have been given nothing at all. Under the pretext of giving, the false teachers had been "taking" their students all along. No wonder they were accused of having "hearts trained in greed" (2 Peter 2:14).

The second letter of Peter points out that loving teachers are those who begin and continue to live as people open to receiving the good news of salvation in Jesus Christ. The author of the letter had not originated the gospel or thought up stories about Jesus. He had received them and, in doing so, refused to put his own interpretation on them. Revelation and interpretation, he confessed, were the work of the Holy Spirit (2 Peter 1:16-21). To be fully instructed in the faith, as he understood it, was to trust that Christ would come again and to anticipate that coming with joy and obedience.

Before they teach, teachers must first receive God's love—to know that they are the beloved. Out of the rich reservoirs of God's love, teachers are prepared to give. Zvi Kolitz claims that the world is divided between givers and takers. The lovers, the ones who are able to live fully, are givers.[2] Having received the gospel, teachers are called to be givers. Theirs is the privilege of opening the Scriptures to those they teach. The church has given to them, in a particular way, the responsibility of identifying, clarifying, and applying what it means to be, by grace, a child of God. It's an awesome responsibility, one that begins with fidelity to what has been received. Exercising this responsibility, one person can give no greater gift to another than the name of Jesus and the witness of faith to his redeeming love.

To love is to anticipate the kingdom of God's love

The false teachers of whom the author of 2 Peter wrote had not been without their expectations. They had allowed them, however, to take the shape of demands—not of themselves but of God. They

105

had shared the views of many in the early church that the ascended Lord Jesus would soon come in power. Not content with the promise, they made his coming a condition for their faith. Then, when Jesus didn't come according to their expectations, they concluded that he wasn't coming at all. They began to scoff at those who continued to trust the promise and developed arguments that justified their position. In 2 Peter it says: "Where is the promise of his coming? For ever since the fathers fell asleep, all things have continued as they were from the beginning of creation" (3:4).

In responding to this challenge the writer of 2 Peter entered into one of the most persistent of debates: is education charged with the task of maintaining the status quo or is it to work for change and equip people to live in a changing world? The false teachers defended the first position. The author of 2 Peter understood this as a denial that God is at work in history and the lives of individuals. Furthermore, it was a justification for the false teachers not to attempt any changes in their lives. Having been denied their expectations, they had none at all—of God, themselves, or others. In the absence of expectations, there is no hope.

The denial of hope is devastating. It encourages the acceptance of whatever conditions people live under, no matter what those are. It leads to a sense of despair and futility—the chilling effects of the meaninglessness of life. It allows for the stereotyping of persons, and even races, that are not at the level of the acceptable status quo, and assigns them at best a second-class existence. Those most willing to *argue* for the unchanging nature of things are most likely to be those who think, though mistakenly, that they have much to lose and nothing to gain through change. Those most willing to *accept* the unchanging nature of things may, however, be those who have been denied the experience of change, and have—in whatever state they live—reconciled themselves to what is. They are the hopeless.

In his refusal to accept hopelessness, the writer of 2 Peter recognized the reality of change. He believed that God is at work in the creation. He trusted in the promise that Jesus would come again in power. That Jesus hadn't come in his lifetime caused him no great problems. God, he maintained, is not limited by the confines of time, as humans are. He quoted the psalmist: "with the Lord one day is as a thousand years, and a thousand years as one day" (2 Peter 3:8). The delay in his coming had nothing to do with his power and everything to do with his love and mercy. God's grace was changing the hearts and lives of people through repentance and faith. Eventually, God would usher in a new age "in which righteousness dwells" (3:8-13). This being God's purpose, who was the writer to question the speed at which the kingdom came?

The author of 2 Peter also recognized the importance of conserving the apostolic tradition and passing it on from one generation to the next. Without that conviction there would have been no need to write his letter. He wouldn't have cared what anyone taught or believed. There could not have been any such thing as a false teacher if there hadn't been something that could be called true. That truth was Jesus. The author of the letter took seriously the necessity of confirming this truth in which the church had been established (2 Peter 1:12-13). What he refused to accept was the relegation of Jesus to a paragraph, a chapter, or even a book in the chronicles of history. He believed that Jesus is alive, and that means that the world has changed and will continue to change. The mission of the church and its teachers is to anticipate the changes of the coming kingdom—the kingdom of the Lord who is love.

To love is to strive for a balance between conserving and change

One of the privileges of teachers is to tell God's story of redemption. Few, if any, would be content without telling the old, old story of Jesus and his love. To know the story and to be able to tell it well, are, in themselves, expressions of a teacher's love. In addition to recounting the content of Scripture and church history, teachers have the responsibility of participating in the activity of

God today. They are called to identify and clarify areas for change, to strive for change in their own lives, and to equip others for the same. At times this may be extremely difficult. Voices may be heard in opposition to the idea that God and the church should be concerned about issues such as hunger, justice, nuclear power, equity, and life. Even where there is a forum in which to discuss these issues, there will undoubtedly be differences of opinion as to how the church should deal with them.

These issues are of Christian concern, because reverence for God leads to love for others. Amos was among the first to argue that case. The first epistle of John makes it clear that love for God leads to involvement in feeding and clothing those who are in need. When Jesus was asked to name the greatest commandment, he responded: love God, and love others. Faith in God leads the disciple into the world to love and to serve.[3]

Teachers will have to wrestle with the meaning of love as it confronts the issues and needs of the day and struggle to fashion a living response to them. In their teaching they will, most likely, find themselves in a variety of roles: confronting, releasing energy, informing, relieving tensions, and generally enabling others to discover and act on the meaning of God's love, and theirs, for the world. Yet to struggle responsibly with the task of enabling change is an expression of one's love for others and of faith that God is working out his purposes for creation.

To love is to acknowledge the value of persons

While the writer of 2 Peter recognized the reality of change in the world, he insisted on both the eternal truth of the gospel and the permanence of the value of persons (2 Peter 3:11). His priority was on a love for people, not things. This is not only a difficult concept to teach others; it's a hard one for teachers to learn as well. It's one that those called to teach have to examine over and over again in their own lives.

Fortunately, volunteer church school teachers aren't caught up in

108

salary negotiations related to their teaching. When there is no monetary compensation for teaching, money cannot become a motivation for doing it. Yet in the ways they spend their energies and invest their talents, teachers have to examine their priorities. Unless teachers know their value as persons, as over against valuing things, they will have difficulty in helping others realize their value.[4]

It's easy to forget that learners are persons and to begin treating them as objects. No one is flattered or helped by that. The problem is, however, that we're not always aware when it is happening. If the followers of the false teachers described in 2 Peter had recognized what was happening to them, what would they have discovered? For one thing, they would have known that they really didn't count as persons. Their only value was in adding to the numbers of those who accepted the opinions of their teachers. By making irreverence and folly popular, the false teachers thought they could make them right. By enticing others into sin, they intended to establish the claim that slavery is really freedom (2 Peter 2:14, 18-19). The false teachers had changed each of their followers from a "thou" into an "it." When people are being used, there is no love.

There are at least four things that teachers can do to assist others in recognizing their value. *The first is to love them as they are.* The author of 2 Peter, much concerned about the effects of the false teachers in their midst, still addresses his readers as "beloved." He wrote to them as ones "who have obtained a faith of equal standing with ours" (2 Peter 1:1; 3:14). There is no patronizing here or putting people down. In his acceptance of them the author reveals the very heart of the gospel. Christ died for all, even when all were sinners. There can be few more powerful testimonies to the gospel than a teacher's acceptance of those who are taught—just as they are.

Second, teachers can be both affirming and critical of those they teach. While affirmation seems to be the most important characteristic of church school teachers, there is room for criticism. The author would not have written the letter he did if he hadn't intended to be critical. He was straightforward in illustrating the errors of false teachers and the consequences for those who followed them. Anything else would have been evidence that he didn't care. But he did care. He realized that love desires the highest good for the beloved.[5] Therefore he wrote a letter that at times is harsh, because he loved those to whom he wrote.

Third, teachers have to expect changes in those they teach. Recent studies have shown that when teachers have no expectations, students don't learn. As true as this may be, one has to be careful. Expectations that are too high are as destructive as none at all. Both fail to take into account students as growing persons.

The writer of 2 Peter expected his readers to examine what he had to say and what they heard from their other teachers. He warned them about the loss of their stability if they failed to grasp, and act on, what he had written. Then, as though in contradiction to what he had just written, he encouraged them to grow in the grace and knowledge of the Lord Jesus (2 Peter 3:17-18). Stability and growth, however, are not contradictory. Together they are a dimension of faith and life. Unless one grows in the understanding of the faith as one grows in the ability to think and act, faith becomes inadequate for living. Unless faith grows with the enlarging spheres of experience that bring successes and failures, joys and sorrows, life and death, faith will not provide the stabilizing power that God intends. Teachers are called to assist their students to grow, and a part of that assistance is to expect it.

At the same time, teachers need to be open to changes in themselves—especially their teaching selves. A friend of mine told of an extremely negative letter he received from one of his students. His first reaction was to throw up his hands in despair and quit. After he got over the initial hurt, he invited the student to talk to him about the letter. As a result of that conversation his teaching style was radically changed. It would be absurd for teachers to expect others to change if *they* are not open to change.

110

Finally, teachers can help students realize their value as persons through the exercise of patience. In a way, it was their lack of patience that was at the root of the problem for the false teachers. They wanted to hurry God. They weren't willing to trust him. That's one kind of impatience. There's another that originates from the love teachers have for their students. Teachers can be so eager for faith and its response that they get frustrated when they see so little evidence of it in the lives of those they teach. Or, anxious for the growth of their students, teachers may look for a more mature faith than it may be reasonable to expect.

But, there is no need, and no way, to hurry faith. In fact, efforts to do so are often counterproductive. After teaching as creatively and conscientiously as they are able, teachers must leave faith and its increase to God. Seen in this light, teaching with patience is more than a ministry that values others as persons. It is a profound expression of faith in God, who values all humankind more than any human teacher could ever imagine or think.

At the beginning of this chapter I acknowledged that 2 Peter was not the most likely text on which to base a discussion of love. Nevertheless, there is love here. The writing of it was, in itself, an act of love. As he drew the letter to a close, the writer remarked about the epistles of Paul. In them, he wrote, there are some things that are hard to understand (3:16). Whatever those hard things might have been, Paul and the writer of 2 Peter would have agreed on this: love is the more excellent way.

Notes

Chapter 1

1. Michael Green, *The Second Epistle General of Peter and the General Epistle of Jude* (London: Tyndale Press, 1968), p. 151.

Chapter 2

1. Richard J. Neuhaus, *Freedom for Ministry* (San Francisco: Harper & Row, 1979), p. 79.
2. Ibid., p. 81.

Chapter 3

1. Lyle Schaller, *Activating the Passive Church: Diagnosis and Treatment* (Nashville: Abingdon, 1981), p. 59.
2. Ibid., p. 47.
3. Ibid., p. 52.
4. Ibid., pp. 79-81.
5. John H. Westerhoff, *Will Our Children Have Faith?* (New York: Seabury, 1976), p. 3.

Chapter 4

1. Edgar M. Carlson, *The Classic Christian Faith* (Minneapolis: Augsburg, 1978), p. 52.
2. David W. Johnson and Roger T. Johnson, *Learning Together and Alone: Cooperative Competition and Individualization* (Englewood Cliffs, NJ: Prentice-Hall, 1975).

Chapter 5

1. Green, p. 69.
2. Elvis Cochrane, *The Epistles of Peter* (Grand Rapids: Baker Book House, 1965), p. 80.

Chapter 6

1. Cochrane, pp. 81-87.
2. Martin Lange and Reinhold Iblacker, eds., *Witnesses of Hope: The Persecution of Christians in Latin America* (Maryknoll, N.Y.: Orbis Books, 1980), p. 5.
3. Cochrane, pp. 81-87.

Chapter 7

1. Geeta and Bernard M. Lall, *Ways Children Learn: What Do Experts Say?* (Springfield: Charles C. Thomas, 1983), pp. 4-6.
2. Sofia Cavaletti, *The Religious Potential of the Child* (New York: Paulist Press, 1979), pp. 21-178.
3. Neuhaus, p. 219.
4. Iris V. Cully, *Christian Child Development* (San Francisco: Harper & Row, 1979), p. 5.
5. Lange and Iblacker, pp. 144-45.
6. Donald B. Rogers, *In Praise of Learning* (Nashville: Abingdon, 1980), p. 26.

Chapter 8

1. G. Johnston, "Love in the New Testament," *The Interpreter's Dictionary of the Bible,* vol. 3, George A. Buttrick, ed. (New York: Abingdon, 1962), p. 174.
2. Zvi Kolitz, *The Teacher: An Existential Approach to the Bible* (New York: Crossroads, 1982), p. 125.
3. Green, p. 70.
4. Ibid., p. 139.
5. Ibid., p. 71.

Appendixes

Appendix A / Securing Teachers
for the Church School

This appendix is intended for use by parish education committees or others responsible for a congregation's educational program as an aid in selecting candidates to teach in the church school. In no way is it intended to set up a board of review over who shall, or shall not, teach. It represents only an effort to determine those in a congregation who seem to be "born" teachers. Recognizing these people becomes a place to start in the selection and training of teachers in order that staff needs for the church school will be met in a consistent and thoughtful manner.

The directions for the discussion are self-explanatory. If the committee has no designated leader, select one before the discussion begins. The leader's responsibilities are to:

1. Read each direction aloud to the group as progress is made through the session.

2. Decide when to move on to the next point in the discussion.

3. Lead the concluding devotion.

Direction sheet

1. The leader states: "We have the responsibility of selecting and inviting people to serve as teachers in our church school. How have we gone about that in the past, and how should we do it?" Allow time for responses. Talk about *why* certain practices have been followed, or why a new method should be implemented.

2. Read aloud Matt. 4:18-20. After reading the passage discuss the following questions:
   a. What word(s) would you use to describe how Jesus "secured" his disciples?
   b. How does Jesus' approach compare with the responses given in Question 1 above?
   c. What are some strengths and problems related to the approach of Jesus when placed into your context?

3. Read aloud Matt. 5:1-2.
   Allow for a few moments of reflection; then read the selection on page 118 entitled "A Basis for Selection." (If possible, the selection could be prerecorded on tape and played back at this time. This would allow for a voice other than the leader's.)

   After reading the selection or listening to the tape, move directly to the next step.

4. Distribute to the group copies of "Teacher Qualifications" (p. 120). Then state: "Here are four statements that could describe favorable characteristics for a Christian teacher. Read over the statements and choose the one that most closely reflects the kind of person you would want to be a teacher in our church school. Think about, and be ready to discuss, the reasons for your choice." Allow five to ten minutes for making choices and reflection.

5. Invite the participants to talk about the choices they made. Possible questions for discussion are:

116

a. Are there any similarities in the choices made?

b. What are the differences in the choices made?

c. How are the differences and similarities accounted for?

d. How important, or unimportant, do you think it is that all teachers have the same qualities?

e. Are there any qualities that you would want all teachers in your school to have? If so, what are they?

6. Think about people in your congregation who presently are not teaching, but seem to have the qualities that make for a good teacher. Who are they? How might they be challenged and encouraged to consider the ministry of teaching?

Allow time for discussion. Decide on a plan of action.

7. Read Matt. 14:22-27 and the following excerpt from *Bless My Growing* by Gerhard Frost (Minneapolis: Augsburg, 1974).

"But I never feel prepared!"
It was at a winter retreat
that a student said it,
and he spoke with the anguish of deep sincerity.
I was pleased when a counselor replied,
"But we walk on water all the time."

It is well to be prepared,
but we dare not forget that we are never fully prepared
for the tasks that are most worth doing.
The tasks that are worthy of us, as persons,
are often beyond us.
This is true of the challenge
of teaching.

Perhaps there is no effort
which is as total,

or which makes one so vulnerable
as teaching.
He who attempts it reaches beyond himself
and senses that his best is not good enough.
Humbling as it is, this work must not discourage us.

As Christians, we who teach
truly walk on water all the time.
It is frightening until one remembers—
remembers and listens—
for across the broad waters comes the voice, saying,
"Fear not, it is I."

Pray the Lord's Prayer.

A basis for selection

Selection was one of the prominent characteristics of the teaching ministry of Jesus. He didn't put an announcement in a bulletin or make a general appeal from a lectern. Jesus selected, or invited, those who were to become his closest disciples. His selections, however, had a larger perspective than the Twelve. He taught them with the intent that they would reach the multitudes. The way to the multitudes was through the preparation of a few who would then go on to bring their witness to Jesus to others. It was critical, therefore, that Jesus choose with care those who would be entrusted with that ministry.

The awareness that Jesus selected his disciples adds great value to whatever ministry one is called to do. As Paul points out in Ephesians 4, and in 1 Corinthians 12, there are varieties of gifts. Listen to what Paul has to say, first from 1 Corinthians 12:

Now there are varieties of gifts, but the same Spirit; and there are varieties of service, but the same Lord; and there are varieties of working, but it is the same God who inspires them all in every one. To each is given the manifestation of the Spirit for the common good. To one is given through the Spirit the

118

utterance of wisdom, and to another the utterance of knowledge according to the same Spirit, to another faith by the same Spirit, to another gifts of healing by the one Spirit, to another the working of miracles, to another prophecy, to another the ability to distinguish between spirits, to another various kinds of tongues, to another the interpretation of tongues. All these are inspired by one and the same Spirit, who apportions to each one individually as he wills (1 Cor. 12:4-11).

And from Ephesians 4:

And his gifts were that some should be apostles, some prophets, some evangelists, some pastors and teachers, to equip the saints for the work of ministry, for building up the body of Christ, until we all attain to the unity of the faith and of the knowledge of the Son of God, to mature manhood, to the measure of the stature of the fulness of Christ; so that we may no longer be children, tossed to and fro and carried about with every wind of doctrine, by the cunning of men, by their craftiness in deceitful wiles. Rather, speaking the truth in love, we are to grow up in every way into him who is the head, into Christ, from whom the whole body, joined and knit together by every joint with which it is supplied, when each part is working properly, makes bodily growth and upbuilds itself in love (Eph. 4:11-16).

As Paul points out, teaching is only one ministry in the life of the church, and not all Christians are expected to be teachers. Yet there can be no doubt that teaching is essential to the life of the church, just as it was essential to Jesus and the preparation of the first disciples. While Jesus followed the practice of selection, or invitation, when it came to gathering these disciples, it is not obvious what principles or qualities guided those selections. The first disciples are a varied lot: a faithful fisherman capable of denial, a loving man who desired a favored place beside his teacher, a tax collector who had once worked for the occupation forces in Israel, at least one doubter, and several who didn't make much of an impression on the pages of the Gospels. Still, all were selected by Jesus to be his disciples.

If it isn't altogether clear what the basis for the selection was, the fact that they were chosen implies the presence of certain qualities in the ones chosen. Today, as one goes about inviting people to serve as teachers in a church school (if that is the practice followed in a particular congregation), the qualities looked for might well be influenced by the biblical and theological outlook, the needs, and the makeup of the congregation involved—as well as the needs of any given class. Keeping in mind our congregation, let's go to the next part of the study.

Teacher qualifications

The Christian teacher is, first of all, a committed Christian who, having a good understanding of the gospel, is dedicated to the task of communicating the gospel to others. In addition, that Christian understanding has been translated into the character and behavior of the teacher in a consistent fashion.

The Christian teacher is one who has an engaging personality. He or she is particularly able to help individuals and groups to deal with issues and problems that stand in the way of the coming kingdom of God. While knowing the Bible is important, the teacher should focus on justice, freedom, and equality for all.

The Christian teacher actively participates in the life of the congregation and does so out of a good knowledge of the biblical and theological tradition of the congregation and denomination. The teacher is "a continually growing person who is becoming more competent in biblical understanding; in the Christian faith; and in active Christian service, fellowship, and worship."

The Christian teacher is one who has gained the necessary skills to effectively teach others about what they are to believe and do as Christians. The teacher should be one who is sensitive to his or her behavior and the behavior of students. As the teacher develops, he or she will learn to control the teaching situation in such a way that students will achieve the desired learning outcomes.

From *An Invitation to Religious Education* by Harold Burgess, © 1975 Religious Education Press, Inc. Used by permission.

Appendix B/Classroom Organization

In their book *Learning Together and Alone,* David and Roger Johnson have described three ways in which teachers can organize a class. They call these organizational patterns goal structures. A goal structure defines the nature of the relationship students have with each other and with the teacher. In this appendix each of the three structures is explained in terms of what it is and the situations in which it is appropriately used. A few examples of activities that can be used in each of the goal structures are also included. This brief summary is only an introduction to the subject. Those responsible for assisting teachers to grow are encouraged to read the source book, which, along with the following outline, could be used as the basis for an in-service training workshop for church school teachers.

I. Individual Goal Structure

    A. *Definition:* an individual goal structure exists when the work and the accomplishments of one student are unrelated to that of other students.

    B. Use it when:
        1. Specific knowledge or skills are to be learned.
        2. There are enough materials for all.
        3. There is adequate space.
        4. There is a minimum standard that all have to attain.
        5. There is a need for freedom from a prescribed schedule.

    C. Some sample activities used in this goal structure:
        1. Worksheets
        2. Study packages
        3. Reading assignments
        4. Homework
        5. Lectures (especially if listeners aren't expected to respond)

II. Competitive Goal Structure

    A. *Definition:* a competitive goal structure exists when students are striving against each other with the result that achieving the goal by one student means that others will not achieve theirs.

B. Use it when:
1. Students are to increase their performance in a speed-related or simple task.
2. The activity takes place in a low-anxiety situation.
3. Students can monitor the progress of their competitors.
4. All participants have the chance of winning.
5. There are clear criteria about right/wrong answers.

C. Some sample activities used in this goal structure:
1. Tests
2. Races
3. Contests
4. Awards
5. Games

III. Cooperative Goal Structure

A. *Definition:* a cooperative goal structure exists when students work together to achieve a goal in common, and where none achieve the objective unless all do.

B. Use it when:
1. Problem solving is desired.
2. Creativity and divergent thinking are encouraged.
3. The objectives are important.
4. The objectives are complex.
5. Developing community and belonging are important.

C. Some sample activities used in this goal structure:
1. Case studies
2. Values clarification
3. Discussion groups
4. Role playing
5. Simulation games

David W. Johnson, Roger T. Johnson, *Learning Together and Alone:* Cooperation, Competition, and Individualization, © 1975, pp. 60-64, 66. Adapted by permission of Prentice-Hall, Inc., Englewood Cliffs, N.J.

Appendix C/Educational Methods

My purpose here is to suggest several alternatives appropriate for each of the four major parts of a lesson plan as described in Chapter 5 and to provide a tool for the discussion of methods among church school teachers.

The following list is intended to be used as an inventory. Copies of it can be made (with other activities listed as desired) and distributed at a teachers' meeting. Ask each teacher to go through it and mark the columns that reflect his or her use and understanding of the methods listed. Compile and discuss the results. This can be done at the meeting where the inventory is taken or at a subsequent gathering. The discussion should include examples and demonstrations of those methods that are unfamiliar to teachers. A chance to practice them would also be helpful.

A part of the presentation on methods could include the reasons why certain methods are used. For example, teachers may have the idea that cutting, pasting, and coloring are fillers that take up the last 10 minutes of a class session. Recognizing that these can be a significant part of a student's learning may make of this a far more important part of the class for both teachers and learners.

I. The Introduction to the Session

    A. The purpose of the introduction
        1. To focus the attention of learners on the subject of the class.
        2. To provide interest in what is to be learned.

B. Some suggested activities	Know	Use	Not familiar
1. Minilecture			
2. Presentation of a hypothetical situation			
3. Reading a current article from a newspaper or magazine			

	Know	Use	Not familiar
4. Showing a picture and asking for a response			
5. Sentence completion			
6. Sharing memories or imaginings			
7. Rating scales			
8. Stories			
9. Games and puzzles			
10. Other			

II. Communication of the New Material

    A. In this part of the session learners are called on to receive the basic content they are to learn. The material may be more or less familiar to them. Once they have received it, they will be asked to think and respond to it. It is assumed that the reflection will be enhanced by what has been learned.

    B. Some suggested activities

	Know	Use	Not familiar
1. Tapes and records			
2. Reading assignments			
3. Worksheets			
4. Questionnaires			
5. Surveys			
6. Observations			
7. Field Trips			
8. Filmstrips			
9. Songs			
10. Movies			
11. Simulation games			
12. Resource persons			
13. Demonstrations			
14. Panels			
15. Debates			

	Know	Use	Not familiar
16. Walks			
17. Telling stories through			
a. Pantomimes			
b. Flannelgraphs			
c. Overheads			
d. Pictures and slides			
e. Puppets			
f. Plays			
g. Speaking			
18. Other			

III. Reflection

A. The purpose for reflection is to address questions such as:
1. Why am I learning this? What's it all about?
2. How does this information fit with what I already know?
3. What changes—if any—do I have to make in my thinking?
4. Is it true? Is it true for me?
5. Do I need to know something more?

B. Some suggested activities:	Know	Use	Not familiar
1. Questions and response			
2. Making a montage, collage, or mobile			
3. Drawing a picture			
4. Writing (telling) a story or poem			
5. Plays or pantomimes			
6. Role playing			
7. Making a movie or slide presentation			

	Know	Use	Not familiar
8. Discussion in twos, threes, or small groups			
9. Values clarification			
10. Case studies			
11. Preparing a program			
12. Other			

IV. Evaluation

   A. The purpose of evaluation is at least two-fold:

      1. For the student it pulls together what the session was all about and provides a basis for affirmation and challenge.

      2. For the teacher it gives insight as to whether or not the objectives were achieved and gives direction for the next session. Evaluation runs through the entire session and involves both the teacher and students.

	Know	Use	Not familiar
B. Some suggested activities:			
1. Observation			
2. Questions (of both teachers and students)			
3. Journals			
4. Sentence completion			
5. Summary statements			
6. Tests			
7. Other			

For Further Reading

Burgess, Harold W. *An Invitation to Religious Education*. Religious Education Press, 1975.

Buttrick, George A. and Crim, Keith R., eds. *The Interpreter's Dictionary of the Bible*. 5 vols. Nashville: Abingdon, 1962.

Carlson, Edgar M. *The Classic Christian Faith*. Minneapolis: Augsburg, 1978. Out of print.

Cavaletti, Sofia. *The Religious Potential of the Child*. New York: Paulist Press, 1979. Out of print.

Cochrane, Elvis. *The Epistles of Peter*. Grand Rapids, MI: Baker Book House, 1965. Out of print.

Cully, Iris V. *Christian Child Development*. San Francisco: Harper & Row, 1979.

Dobson, James. *Dare to Discipline,* Wheaton, IL: Tyndale, 1970.

Eaton, Evelyn and Whitehead, James D. *Christian Life Patterns: The Psychological Challenges and Religious Invitations of Adult Life.* NY: Doubleday, 1982.

Everist, Norma J. *Education Ministry in the Congregation*. Minneapolis: Augsburg, 1983.

Gordon, Thomas. *Teacher Effectiveness Training*. Wyden, 1975.

Green, Michael. *Second Epistle Peter and the Epistle of Jude*. Tyndale Bible Commentaries: Vol. 18. Grand Rapids, MI: Eerdmans, 1968.

268
067 7577

Johnson, David W. and Johnson, Roger T. *Learning Together and Alone: Cooperation Competition and Individualization.* Englewood Cliffs, NJ: Prentice-Hall, 1975.

Kerr, John, ed. *Teaching Grades Seven through Ten.* Parish Life, 1980. Out of print.

Kolitz, Zvi. *The Teacher: An Existential Approach to the Bible.* New York: Crossroads, 1982.

Kreider, Eugene. *I Want to Be a Teacher.* Minneapolis: Augsburg, 1981.

Lall, Geeta and Bernard M. *Ways Children Learn: What Do Experts Say?* Springfield, IL: Charles C. Thomas, 1982.

Lange, Martin and Iblacker, Reinhold, eds. *Witnesses of Hope: The Persecution of Christians in Latin America.* Maryknoll, NY: Orbis Books, 1981.

Neuhaus, Richard J. *Freedom for Ministry.* San Francisco: Harper and Row, 1979.

Rogers, Donald B. *In Praise of Learning.* Nashville: Abingdon, 1980. *Parish Teacher Annual,* vol. 5. Minneapolis: Augsburg, 1981.

Schaller, Lyle. *Activating the Passive Church: Diagnosis and Treatment.* Nashville: Abingdon, 1981.

Westerhoff, John H. *Will Our Children Have Faith?* New York: Seabury, 1976. Out of print.

Westerhoff, John H. and Willimon, William H. *Liturgy and Learning Through the Life Cycle.* New York: Seabury, 1980.

Wilson, Marlene. *How to Mobilize Church Volunteers.* Minneapolis: Augsburg, 1983.